Eating for Energy
Four Seasons of Real Food

KATHY *Parry*
Your Real Food Coach

Eating for Energy
Four Seasons of Real Food

A Kathy Parry Book

Writing & Publishing Process by PlugAndPlayPublishing.com

Photography & Front Cover Design by Nancy Koch

Back Cover Design by Tracey Miller | www.TraceOfStyle.com

Edited by Lauren Cullumber

ISBN: 1517267412

EAN-13: 978-1517267414

Disclaimer:

This book contains opinions, ideas and experiences and is not intended as medical and/or health advice. Please consult a medical professional before adopting any of the suggestions in this book. The purchaser and/or reader of these materials assumes all responsibility for the use of this information. Kathy Parry and Publisher assume no responsibility and/or liability whatsoever for any purchaser and/or reader of these materials.

For My Parents: Nancy and Stuver Parry
Amazing role models and the source of my inspiration for this book.

Dad you grew the most beautiful garden that instilled a love of real food.

Mom I miss you every day but I am thankful that you allowed me to mess up your kitchen which fostered my love of cooking.

Contents

Introduction

I grew up in a garden. Really. Some of my earliest memories include asparagus spears popping through the spring soil, peppers eaten right off the plant, and carrots pulled from a sandy patch of dirt. My father had a half-acre organic garden back in the 1970s and it was an open playground and snack bar all rolled up in one sweet smelling patch of earth.

Early each spring, all my siblings and I were given garden prep chores. Shoveling manure onto the beds, helping Dad tie strings to mark each row to be hoed, dropping the seeds into the neatly marked rows and even draping the cherry tree in cheesecloth to keep the birds away! My father was committed to growing our food without chemicals. (I later learned this was because my mother told him she didn't want chemicals in our food.) But one of my favorite parts of this gardening style was the day the bugs arrived. Little boxes came in the mail and my dad was so excited to open them. We didn't know what they held, but as he peeled back the brown paper, small pods were revealed. Mail order praying mantis and lady bug eggs were part of his pesticide protocol.

After prepping the garden in the spring, we went into full-blown vegetable harvesting mode in the summer. Before I could go to the pool I picked beans. Before dinner I sat in front of the television and shelled peas. And before bed I ate a big piece of cherry pie. While it was my father who grew the vegetables, it was my mother who was charged with making them delicious.

I'm not saying the rutabaga was delicious by a kid's standards, but the sweet corn soufflés, wilted spinach salads, black raspberry cobblers, cucumbers in sour cream with chives, and zucchini casserole formed my palate for vegetables. My mother canned tomatoes, froze bushels of green beans and packed grocery bags full of vegetables to share with friends. I cannot think of my childhood without picturing my mother in the kitchen preparing food with reverence. Food was respected and elevated in our home.

That all happened when I was young. It wasn't until I was older that I fell in love with the garden in a year-round kind of way. I learned to cook. I was the youngest of four children and the kitchen became a really good source of entertainment. While my older siblings were off at college or soccer camp, I hung out in the kitchen with my mother. Sifting and rolling and stirring were all great fun. As a ten-year-old I made French Onion Soup, just because I wanted it. And a funny thing happened. My mother started to step out of the kitchen. She had been cooking for a lot of years and dealing with those huge summer harvests. But as my siblings needed her less and less, she left the kitchen for garden club and a part time job. That left me lots of time to experiment. Pretty soon I took over several meals a week.

Recipes for me were always guidelines. The kitchen was really meant for creating. This spirit of creation lead me to minor in food management in college and work at specialty food markets while I continued to kindle my love of seasonal foods. While going to school in a small town in Ohio, I actually found a farmers market where I could buy local tomatoes and apples on those cool September mornings. My housemates couldn't believe I owned a rolling pin and that I made an apple pie in our ill-equipped kitchen. When I began seriously cooking on my own after college I was always looking for the foods of my youth: the produce. Meat, yeah it was fine, but give me an acorn squash and that was a greater challenge. I could stuff it with dried cherries and fresh thyme. Or maybe a farmhouse cheddar cheese and sage. I would dream of flavor combinations and my creations always included fruits and vegetables. It's not difficult to figure out why that by my early thirties, I had forgone meat completely.

My love for cooking and the seasonal produce of my youth led me to create this book. I am a food coach and professional speaker and I am constantly asked for recipes. What are the right foods to eat? Or, how do I feed a vegetarian? This book didn't start out as a vegetarian book, but that's how it ended up. Eating for energy involves a lot of different foods and that is explained more in the next chapter. This book is a culmination of a lifetime love for seasonal foods. Yes, I get excited over the apples of fall, the peas of spring and the parsnips of winter. Something about eating for each season seems the best way to enjoy our food. And eating the right foods for your health just happens to include all these delicious fruits and vegetables. I hope you enjoy this taste journey through the seasons. I honor my childhood, my parents and my love of living an energetic life in each recipe.

Chapter 1
Eating for Energy and
The REAL Food Revolution

So, yes this book is about seasonal cooking, but why energy? What is that all about? After working with thousands of people, I know that most people only want a few things when it comes to making healthful changes. First, they want to lose weight. That is kind of an obvious place to start because the majority of Americans are carrying around a bulge or bump or jiggle that they don't want. But the second thing I always hear is, "I wish I had more energy." I have written a whole book about having more energy! ***The Ultimate Recipe for an Energetic Life*** is my book that describes exactly why we are low on energy and how simple changes in our diet can help us live a more energetic life. **I would love for you to head over to Amazon.com right now and order yourself a copy!** Really. This book will give you the information you need about your energy levels, your amazing cells and the many reasons why your eyes get heavy every afternoon.

My passion for helping people live their most energetic lives is inspired by the youngest of my four children. Merritt Joy does not properly process food into energy. The mitochondria in her cells don't function properly. My journey with Merritt and her diagnosis are documented in my first book. But summarizing her diagnosis is important to what you will learn in this book. Merritt's doctors told me she would only live for two years because of her wonky cells (wonky is not a medical term...just mine). But when the doctors gave me this news, all I heard was "food and energy." With my background in food and my love of real food, I set out to find out how to feed her cells so she could process foods. My poor baby was sleeping 18-24 hours a day, even at a year old. After I changed her diet to a vegan, no gluten, no dairy diet, she woke up! Literally she had more energy. And although she is highly disabled from her disease, Merritt is fourteen now, and a very healthy child!

Fifty percent of our energy every day goes to the process of digesting food and getting it into our cells. So yes, there are foods that you eat that rob you of energy because they are difficult to break down and digest. And conversely, some foods break down easily, requiring minimal energy, therefore giving you left over energy for running circles around your day! If you eat a mostly plant-based diet with minimal sugar and simple carbohydrates, you will feel more energetic. Your body will get the nutrients it needs in order to convert food into energy in the cells.

I want you to live your most energetic life! I want your cells to process food properly and make you mountains of fabulous energy so you can live a big, bold life. And this book contains the recipes that will help you on your way.

What Is REAL Food?

When I speak to organizations and companies I use the term "whole real food." I was happily going along saying this at corporate presentations until one day someone raised their hand and said, "What is a whole, real food?" Oops. I forgot that not everyone grew up picking beans.

A whole real food is a food in its unaltered state. It is an orange. It is a head of broccoli. It is an egg. It is a farm-raised chicken. It is a food that has not been processed in any way. So a box of Sun Dried Tomato Wheat Crackers may sound like a whole real food, but it isn't. It is a package of highly processed food. This book aims to use ingredients in their whole, real form and transform them into delicious dishes. When the sum of the parts come together, you will have food that supports your cells' functions and makes energy in your body. (And if you want to know what those chemicals in fake food do...go order my other book!)

What Is In This Book?

Seasonal Sections: As I mentioned earlier, I am passionate about seasonal eating. So this cookbook is laid out by season. That isn't to say that you can't have *Green Beans with Walnuts and Lemon* in the winter, even though they are listed in the summer section. Go for it. Mix it up if you like. But I tried to pick recipes inspired by the foods of each season. Of course we live in a world that provides us with grocery stores that stock tomatoes and cucumbers year round. But for the most part, try to buy what is in season in your region, or at least somewhere in the United States. When foods travel from around the world they lose nutrients, and we have no clue about the farming techniques used in Ecuador.

Simple Methods: I tried really hard to make the methods and techniques easy for even basic cooks to master. Fancy cooking terms can be reserved for the Food Network Chefs. But if you ever have a question about a particular recipe or method to get it produced, email me. Really. I answer emails. And typos happen. Go on, try me at: Kathy@KathyParry.com

Variety: When we're used to eating over-processed foods or recipes that rely on animal protein, we don't try new things. We get stuck in ruts. This book has recipes with influences from a host of cuisines. You will find recipes inspired by flavors of Mexico, India, Thailand, Italy, and other countries with different spice profiles. If you don't have the spices listed, don't stress. You can always leave a spice out. But variety is the spice of life!

Fat: Yes, you will find butter in this book. Also olive oil and coconut oil. I like fat. Fat is good for your cells. I don't overdo it with fats, but good healthy fats are a necessary part of your diet. So don't get too freaked out by a little butter. It comes from a cow and is a real food. Margarine, Crisco and corn and canola oils are not on my list of fats to use. Again, you can learn the reasons behind this in my first book.

Salt: Yep, too much salt can be dangerous to your health. Amounts of salt in my recipes are kept pretty low, but as a cook I always season to taste. I invite you to do the same. Start with a small amount of salt and taste before adding more. And all of my recipes call for sea salt. Sea salt, especially grey or pink, has all its minerals intact. It hasn't been heated and processed like regular industrial table salt. So even when you're using sea salt, you're getting some nutritional value.

Reasonable Portions: Look at the portions mentioned in each recipe. These are realistic. Making an entire recipe of *Mushroom and Spinach Ragu* for two people means you've portioned too much. Portion control is a major factor in the increase of obesity in America. Start small, then wait fifteen minutes. If you're still hungry, have a few more bites. And try not to fall into the trap I do. When I do the dishes I eat more straight from the pan. This is a good reason to get your kids or spouse to do the dishes!

Organic Stuff: For the most part I encourage you to seek out organic produce. But some organic produce is grown using methods that are really similar to non-organic, the chemicals are just a bit better for you. I call this *Big Organic Farming*. The other type of organic farming is the type I really think is best for your health. This is *Local Organic Farming*. Knowing your farmer or at least the region your food is from is really a great practice. Not only do you benefit from a low chemical exposure, local organic or small farm organics usually tend their soil with great nutrients like manure and natural mulch. But I realize many of us live in areas with a short growing season and local ingredients don't last too long. And yes, organics can be more expensive. You may not have access to organic. So don't sweat it. Whenever we can reduce our chemical profile we should try. You will see that anytime I mention a packaged product like black beans or Greek yogurt I typically say "organic" in front of it. In my first book I devote a whole chapter to "Fake Food" and why eating chemicals isn't a great idea for an energetic life. So try your best to use organic, but no matter, eating more vegetables in *any* form is healthier than fried pork rinds.

Canned Foods: Yes, some recipes call for canned foods. I know not everyone has time to make vegetable stock. You will find recipes that call for canned beans, canned tomatoes and canned broths. These are all time consuming items to make from scratch. (Although I do encourage you to try it, especially beans. Dried beans are delicious, and cheap, too.) I encourage you to look for organic varieties of anything you are buying in a can. And really read the labels; you don't want to see added junk. Look out for anything that says "natural flavors" as this is code for MSG. And sugar sneaks into a lot of tomato products. Just look before leaping on the canned goods.

What Isn't In This Book?

Dessert: I was so torn on having a dessert section. The first thing you must understand: processed sugar does not create energy in the cells. Refined sugar, yes the white stuff used in most desserts, damages cells, leads to disease and accelerates aging. So how would I put desserts in this book? I struggled. I could make black bean and date brownies. I've done that before. But honestly, I don't eat many desserts and if I do, then I want real dessert. Like homemade peach pie. Or bittersweet chocolate brownies. So I finally decided, "No desserts in this book!" And then I had such a sense of relief. I really didn't want to make "healthy" desserts, because I don't believe in them. They still have some form of sugar. If you want desserts and sweets there are a load of places to find them. Just look for real ingredients and keep portion sizes small.

Meat: If you haven't figured it out yet, this is a vegetarian cookbook. I have been a vegetarian for almost 20 years. My daughter is a vegan. Vegan means no animal products at all...eggs, cheese or dairy. This works for her. (But I like a little cheese and eggs and oh yeah...half and half in my decaf!) My goal is not to turn you into a vegetarian, although you may find it is the best change you've ever made!

To learn even more about my daughter's condition and how I could help others feel their best, I became certified in plant-based nutrition from T. Colin Campbell, the Cornell University professor and author of *The China Project*. My course work helped me further validate the importance of eating a plant-based diet and eliminating animal protein.

Meat is difficult to digest. And as Americans we eat way too much. We just don't need the amount of animal protein that we currently consume. Our cells need nutrients, including protein, but we can get that protein from plant sources. So if you need meat, okay. Add any meat to any recipe or go get your recipes from Bobby Flay or Michael Simon (he's the celebrity chef with a pig tattoo). And if you find that you need to cook for a vegetarian, you now have an excellent source of inspiration in these pages!

Gluten: "Do I have to go gluten-free?" That is a question I get asked ALL the time. The answer is probably not. Gluten is the protein found in grains, and most abundantly in flour. And we love white flour in this country. The majority of us can process gluten, but, and here's the kicker, not easily. Gluten is hard to digest. And we run into problems because of the longevity of our gluten habit. When we're young we may digest it fine. But over time, systems break down. Then gluten starts leaking through tiny holes in our digestive track. This syndrome, known as leaky gut, leads to a host of diseases and general lousy feelings.

When my daughter was a year old and I read all the research on gluten, I decided it was time for her to kick that habit. Do you have to kick it too? Unless you've been diagnosed with a gluten sensitivity or show signs of gastrointestinal stress, I say, "just reduce it." And to make that easy on you, I've included almost no gluten in this book. And especially no white flour. But you will find a recipe for an awesome *Sweet Potato Crusted Pizza* to fulfill that need.

Tons of Dairy: I've tried to limit the dairy profile in these recipes. Because like gluten, many people have a hard time digesting the proteins in dairy foods. You may not have been diagnosed with any specific issues, but rather you may bloat, have indigestion or diarrhea after eating dairy. When these symptoms happen, it means your body is working hard just to repair the damage being done by dairy. You can't feel energetic if you are in digestive distress. You also won't get the nutrients from the food if you aren't digesting it well. But no cheese? Really? Living without some cheese is just rough.

What Is Here Or What Isn't?

One concept I try to avoid when coaching people is that of deprivation. No one wants to think they are getting something taken away. So I would really encourage you not to think about the foods that aren't in this book. Instead I want you to think about the crispest apple you've ever eaten in the fall. I want you to remember the flavor of your grandmother's vegetable soup on a cold winter night. And think about the first time you tried an artichoke in the spring! (If you haven't had a fresh artichoke, put that on your bucket list!)

Are you ready to experience a higher level of energy and health? Are you ready to make a plan and take the time to make some real food? (I don't come to your kitchen and cook any of this!) Then get your browsing eyes ready and flip the page! Let's get cooking so you can start feeling your most energetic.

Chapter 2

Spring

Spring is hope and anticipation all rolled up in the smell of dirt. I walk around my flower garden in the spring begging the first daring perennials to show their tender green shoots. Foods in the spring should mimic this feeling of new and green. You'll find peas, sweet onions, spinach and mint in these recipes. As we emerge from colder months, we crave lighter, fresher and greener foods.

Beginnings and Apps

Chipotle Hummus

Tomato and Queso Fresco with Chimichurri Sauce

Quinoa Tabbouleh

Spinach Artichoke Dip with Sunflower Seeds
and Roasted Red Peppers

Chipotle Hummus

Spice level for this uniquely flavored hummus can be adjusted by the number of chipotles and sauce that you add. Two peppers makes it mildly spicy, three and you may have to warn anyone who eats it that there is some heat! Serve with cucumber slices or a healthier-version tortilla like flax seed tortillas.

1 15 oz can organic garbanzo beans

2 cloves garlic

2-3 canned chipotle peppers with adobe sauce

½ cup organic tahini

½ cup water

Juice of one lemon

2 TBS olive oil

½ tsp. salt

Combine the garbanzo beans, chipotles and garlic in the bowl of a food processor or powerful blender. Pulse until well chopped and becoming smooth. Add the tahini, water, lemon juice, olive oil and salt and continue to process until very smooth. Serve immediately. Makes 2 cups.

This can be refrigerated for 4-5 days. However once chilled the hummus does become less creamy as the fats solidify.

Tomato and Queso Fresco
with Chimichurri Sauce

This is a Mexican/South American version of the Italian Caprese appetizer. Instead of pesto and mozzarella this spicy version uses mild queso fresco cheese with spicy chimichurri. This sauce originated in Argentina as a condiment to meat, but I love it on vegetables and as flavor-kick to this appetizer.

48 cherry tomatoes

8 oz queso fresco – find it in the Mexican section of the refrigerated area

24 leaves of cilantro

1 recipe Chimichurri – see below

Cut the queso into 24 cubes. On toothpicks or skewers layer a tomato, piece of cheese, leaf of cilantro and another tomato. Arrange on a platter with a bowl of chimichurri.

Chimichurri Sauce

1 cup of packed cilantro leaves

2 cups of packed parsley leaves

5-10 slices of jarred jalapeno slices or 1 small fresh jalapeno (depending on how spicy you like it)

3 cloves of garlic, peeled

½ cup olive oil

1/3 cup red wine vinegar

½ tsp. sea salt

In the bowl of a food processor, pulse the cilantro, parsley, garlic and jalapeno until fine. Scrape down the sides. With the machine running, add the olive oil, vinegar and salt. Process until well combined. The chimichurri won't be perfectly smooth, but it should not have any big chunks of herbs. Makes 1 ½ cups.

Quinoa Tabbouleh

Traditionally tabbouleh is made with cracked wheat, called bulghur. But as many of us try to move away from eating a lot of wheat, due to the often difficult to digest gluten, quinoa makes an excellent substitute. I actually like it better than bulghur. And of course mint is usually popping up by mid-April in most herb gardens.

1 cup quinoa cooked according to package directions, yield about 2 cups

1 large English cucumber, diced

1 ½ cups chopped tomatoes

2 cups parsley, chopped

1 cup mint, chopped

2 cloves garlic, minced

½ cup olive oil

Juice from 2 lemons

½ tsp. salt

½ tsp. pepper

Cool the cooked quinoa in a large bowl. Toss in the cucumbers and tomatoes. Stir well to combine. Add the parsley, mint, garlic, olive oil, lemon juice, salt and pepper. Stir very well to combine. The flavors in the tabbouleh come out as it sits for a bit. So serving it the next day works well for this salad. Serves 6-8.

Spinach Artichoke Dip with Sunflower Seeds and Roasted Red Peppers

Spinach and artichokes are some of the first domestic crops of the spring. Spinach artichoke dip has been around forever. And this iconic dip is crying for a makeover. Unfortunately the kind you order at a chain restaurant or have at a tailgate party is loaded with processed mayonnaise and cheese. Ugh. Who says this fan-favorite has to be junked up? Enjoy this version with a nutrient-filled chip like one made with quinoa or flax seeds.

4 cups fresh spinach (or 1 package frozen, defrosted and squeezed dry)

1 cup chopped kale

1 12 oz jar marinated artichokes

1 12 oz jar roasted red peppers

½ cup raw unsalted sunflower seeds

3 cloves garlic

½ tsp sea salt

½ tsp black pepper

¼ cup plain Greek yogurt

1 TBS organic mayonnaise

Preheat the oven to 350 degrees. Lightly steam the fresh spinach in a pan with a small amount of water or in a glass bowl in the microwave, just until it is wilted. (If you're using frozen spinach you do not need to cook it.) Squeeze the water out of the spinach. Place the spinach, kale, artichokes, roasted red peppers, garlic and sunflower seeds in the bowl of a food processor. Pulse the mixture until it is roughly chopped. Add the salt, pepper, yogurt, and mayonnaise and pulse just to combine. Place the dip in an oven-proof baking dish. Bake in the preheated oven for 30 - 40 minutes. Allow the dip to cool for 20 minutes before serving. This is even great cold the next day. Makes about 3 cups.

Beverages

Mint Cucumber Water with Aloe Juice Splash

Coconut Water with Strawberries and Lime

Detox Smoothie with Lemon, Mango and Cucumber

Strawberry, Mint and Aloe Juice Smoothie

Mint Cucumber Water with Aloe Juice Splash

Mint is not just for mint juleps on Derby Day! Mint is abundant in gardens in the spring and it is refreshing in this water. Add cucumbers and aloe for their detoxifying effects on your liver.

1 quart purified or spring water

½ cucumber, sliced thin

½ cup mint leaves, muddled

1 cup aloe juice

To muddle mint, place it in a bowl and smash a bit with a spoon or use a mortar and pestle to smash. Don't over smash so that it turns mushy or falls apart. Muddling allows the essential oils to release from the mint. Combine all the ingredients in a large pitcher. Chill the water overnight for best flavors. Serve over ice. Makes 4 servings.

Coconut Water with Strawberries and Lime

Coconut water is loaded with trace minerals that are essential for good cellular health. Look for a coconut water without sugar or additives. This is an excellent water to drink after a workout as the coconut water naturally replaces electrolytes.

---

2 cups purified or spring water

2 cups coconut water

1 cup sliced strawberries

1 lime sliced thin

Combine all the ingredients in a large pitcher. Chill the water overnight for the best flavors. Serve over ice. Makes 4 servings.

Detox Smoothie with Lemon, Mango and Cucumber

Something about spring makes us want to clean. Why not clean your insides too! Lemon juice stimulates the liver to make extra enzymes. This helps your body detox chemicals more effectively. Parsley, pineapple, cucumber and mango are all detox boosters too.

1 cup pineapple chunks

½ cup cucumber chunks

½ cup mango chunks (fresh or frozen)

½ cup parsley

Juice from ½ lemon

2 -3 ice cubes

Blend on high speed until smooth. Makes 1 serving

Strawberry, Mint and Aloe Juice Smoothie

Strawberries are abundant in the spring and oh so good in a smoothie! Aloe juice is purifying and the mint is refreshing. Baby kale is not as bitter as regular kale yet has all the same nutrients.

1 cup fresh strawberries

1 cup baby kale

¼ cup fresh mint leaves

½ cup aloe juice

4 ice cubes

Blend on high speed until smooth. Makes 1 serving

Salads

Lentil Salad with Chive Vinaigrette

Black Bean Avocado Salad

Warm Spring Lentil Salad with Asparagus and Fennel

Quinoa with Peas, Dill and Feta

Spinach Salad with Strawberries, Mangos,
Pistachios, Feta and Mint

Lentil Salad with Chive Vinaigrette

Chives are one of the first herbs to pop up in my herb garden. And while they add an onion flavor, it never comes across as strong as an onion. And adding the spinach to the dressing gives a big nutrient punch to this dressing that screams spring.

1 cup green lentils – I like French lentils because they stand up well in a salad

1 cup chopped tomatoes

1 cup chopped cucumbers

2 large carrots, chopped

½ cup chopped fresh chives

Cook the lentils in about 2 cups of water in a saucepan over medium heat. Most lentils take about 20-30 minutes. Put the lentils in a bowl and stick the bowl in the freezer for 10-15 minutes to cool them more quickly. Meanwhile chop the rest of the ingredients and make the dressing recipe below. Add the chopped vegetables to the cooled lentils and toss in the salad dressing. Makes 6 servings.

Spinach Chive Dressing

4 cups of baby organic spinach

½ cup chives

½ cup olive oil

¼ cup red wine vinegar

2 TBS balsamic vinegar

½ tsp sea salt

Combine all the ingredients in a powerful blender. Blend until smooth. Makes about 1 cup.

Black Bean Avocado Salad

No matter where you live in the country, fresh avocados seem to make their way to most grocery stores year round due to a consistent growing season in South America. But California avocados start coming on strong in the spring months here in the US. This is a simple salad to whip up in a matter of minutes.

1 can organic black beans or garbanzo beans, drained

1 avocado, diced

1 cup kale, chopped fine

¼ cup raw pepitas (pumpkin seeds)

1 cup cherry tomatoes, halved or whole

2 TBS olive oil

Juice of ½ lime

½ tsp cumin

Salt and pepper to taste

Combine everything in a bowl...easy, easy. Serves 2-4 depending on if it is a side or main course.

Warm Spring Lentil Salad with Asparagus and Fennel

When spring seems to be just around the corner it is time to break out the flavors that have been dominated by stews and heavy flavors. Delicate dill and crisp asparagus are both early risers in the spring garden. And by adding the zest of the lemon you gain not only flavor but powerful detoxifying agents from the oils in the peel.

1 cup French green lentils

2 cups water

1 6 oz bag organic baby spinach, chopped into ½ inch pieces

2 TBS olive oil for roasting

1 medium onion, chopped

1 whole fennel bulb, chopped in ½ inch pieces

1 bunch asparagus, tough bottoms removed, and sliced into 1 inch pieces

Zest from one lemon

Juice from one lemon

½ tsp. garlic powder

¼ tsp salt

½ tsp pepper

¼ cup chopped fresh dill

½ cup feta

1-2 TBS extra virgin olive oil to top salad

Put the 2 cups of water and 1 cup of lentils in a medium sauce pan over medium heat. Bring the lentils to a boil and then reduce to a simmer. Simmer the lentils until al dente, about 20-30 minutes. You may have to add a touch more water depending on your lentils. (I like the green French lentils known as LePuy because they hold their shape and don't become mushy). Once the lentils seem almost done, stir the chopped spinach into the lentils. Stir on and off for five minutes until the spinach wilts and cooks. Remove lentils and spinach from the stove and transfer to a medium bowl to cool.

Preheat oven to 425 degrees. Coat a baking sheet with the 2 TBS with olive oil. Toss the fennel, onion and asparagus in the olive oil on the baking sheet. Sprinkle with salt and pepper. Roast the vegetables in the oven for 10 minutes, stir the vegetables and roast another 10 minutes. Veggies should be a little brown on the edges. Remove from the oven and cool.

When vegetables are room temperature, pour them into the lentils. Stir in the lemon zest, lemon juice, garlic powder, salt, pepper, fresh dill and feta. Stir the salad together and drizzle 1 – 2 TBS olive oil over the salad. Serve at room temperature or chill and serve later. Serves 4-6.

Quinoa with Peas, Dill and Feta

I took this to a luncheon in early April and it was a big hit! By that time of year everyone is tired of winter food and this is a perfect salad to start off spring. Add a piece of grilled chicken or salmon for non-vegetarians. The quinoa really fluffs up so this will serve more than you may think.

1 cup quinoa, cooked according to package directions

2 stalks celery, chopped

2 cups chopped cucumber

2 cups finely chopped kale

1 bag frozen organic peas

½ cup chopped dill

Zest from one lemon

1 cup crumbled feta

Cook the quinoa according to package directions. Transfer to a bowl and add the frozen peas.

Put it in all in the refrigerator for a few minutes to cool. Meanwhile chop the kale and the dill very fine. Remove the quinoa from the refrigerator and add the celery, kale, cucumber, dill, zest and feta.

Dressing:

2/3 cup extra virgin olive oil

Juice from one lemon

1 tsp. Dijon mustard

2 TBS apple cider vinegar

In a small jar with a lid, combine the dressing ingredients and shake. Pour over the salad. Serves 6-8.

Spinach Salad with Strawberries, Mangos, Pistachios, Feta and Mint

The mint in this salad makes the whole thing come alive! And spring is the perfect time to throw mint in everything. Use raw honey in the salad dressing if you have it. This version of the sweet stuff has great anti-viral properties to help ward off a spring virus.

6 cups fresh baby spinach

1 cup sliced organic strawberries

1 cup cubed mango

½ cup feta cheese

½ cup pistachios (raw)

½ cup fresh mint leaves chopped

Raw Honey Balsamic Dressing:

½ cup olive oil

¼ cup balsamic vinegar

2 tsp. red wine vinegar

1 TBS raw honey

Dash of salt

Toss all salad ingredients in a large bowl. Combine dressing ingredients in a glass jar with a lid and shake well. Start with about ½ the dressing and toss with salad. If you need more, add until your desired dressing quota is met! Serves 4-6

Soups

Black Bean, Kale and Quinoa Soup with Cilantro Cream

Spicy Cold Cucumber Soup with Avocados

Potato Leek Soup

Lentil and Carrot Soup with Ginger

Black Bean, Kale and Quinoa Soup with Cilantro Cream

I'm a huge fan of black bean soup, but sometimes straight up black beans feel predictable. In attempt to change it up, I added a few more super foods and some spice and came up with this amazing rendition. Beans offer a triple bonus as a super food. They have fiber, protein and phytonutrients! Win, win, win!

2 TBS olive oil

3 cloves garlic, chopped

1 large onion, chopped

2 large carrots, peeled and chopped

2 stalks celery, chopped

1 yellow bell pepper, chopped

1, 4 oz. can green chilis or one fresh chili pepper like an Anaheim

2, 15 oz cans organic chopped tomatoes

2, 15 oz cans organic black beans, rinsed in a colander

1 -2 chipotle peppers in adobe sauce (these are canned)

2-3, 15 oz cans filled with water

3 cups chopped kale

1 TBS cumin

1 TBS chili powder

1 tsp each salt and pepper

½ cup quinoa

1 avocado, chopped

In a 2 quart or larger pot, heat the olive oil over medium heat on the stove top. Add the garlic and onion. Cook, stirring for five minutes until onions begin to turn translucent. Add the carrots, celery, pepper, chilis and cook, stirring five more minutes. Add remaining ingredients, EXCEPT quinoa. Bring to a simmer and then turn soup down to low. Cook over low heat for 1 ½ hours. After 1 ½ add the ½ cup quinoa. Simmer over low for an additional 30-45 minutes. I like my soups a bit smoother so I use an immersible hand blender and blend the soup for just a few seconds. You can also use a blender or food processor, but it is messy. This step is optional. Serve the soup with the cilantro cream (recipe below), and chopped avocados.

Note: Chipotle peppers will give this soup a kick. If you don't like spicy, you may want to omit them. The chipotle mellows and often isn't as spicy the next day.

Cilantro Cream

½ cup unflavored Greek yogurt

¼ cup chopped cilantro

2 tsp. lime juice (approximately ¼ lime juiced)

1/8 tsp. salt

Combine all ingredients in a small bowl and stir. It is best to do this while the soup is cooking so the flavors can combine.

Spicy Cold Cucumber Soup with Avocados

This isn't your mother's garden party cold soup. I love cold cucumber soup, but I like a little more flavor. So this one has some added spice with some jalapeno. If you don't like spice, add a half cup of fresh dill. Then your mother may like it! And adding arugula or spinach gives it a more powerful nutrient punch.

2 stalks celery, rough chopped

1 large English cucumber, rough chopped

2 scallions, rough chopped

5 jarred jalapeno slices or ½ fresh jalapeno

1 cup packed arugula or spinach leaves

1/2 cup water

1 cup plain Greek yogurt

1 tsp sea salt

1 tsp black pepper

½ avocado, diced

1 cup cherry tomatoes, quartered

In a powerful blender, like a Vitamix, combine the celery, cucumber, scallions, jalapeno, arugula, and water. Blend until very smooth. Transfer to a bowl and add the Greek yogurt, salt, pepper and whisk vigorously to combine. In 4 individual bowls place some diced avocado and tomatoes. Ladle soup over the avocado and tomatoes. Serves 4.

Potato Leek Soup

These classic flavors are perfect for a chilly spring night. Leeks make the soup sweet and potatoes keep it hardy. For a different flavor, add broccoli and cheddar...your kids will go wild for it. Serve it with a spinach salad and you've doubled up the vitamins.

2 TBS butter

3 large leeks, bottom half, sliced in ½ and cut in semi-circles

1 cup chopped onion

1 ½ pounds yellow potatoes, like Yukon Gold, skin on, chopped

2 large carrots, diced

1 quart vegetable stock

1 cup water

Salt and pepper to taste

Shredded cheddar cheese (optional)

In a medium large pot, melt the butter over medium heat. Add the leeks and onions to the pot. Sauté for 5-8 minutes, stirring. Once leeks and onions begin to soften, add the potatoes and carrots. Sauté for another 5-8 minutes until beginning to soften. Add the stock and water. Simmer the soup for 30 minutes. Add additional water if it becomes too thick. Season with salt and pepper. Puree the soup using a hand-held immersible blender or transfer soup to a blender. Process until desired consistency. Makes 4-6 servings.

Lentil and Carrot Soup with Ginger

Carrot and ginger are a classic combination, but a carrot puree soup with ginger has a high natural sugar content that can spike insulin. Turning this flavor into a lentil soup adds fiber and protein. Ginger is a natural digestive aid. Curl up with a bowl on a rainy spring day.

1 cup lentils

4 cups vegetable broth

2 cups water

2 cups chopped carrots – about 4 large

1 cup chopped onion

1 cup chopped mushrooms

1 cup chopped kale

1 TBS fresh grated ginger

1 tsp ground ginger

1 tsp garlic powder

1 tsp cardamom

1 ½ tsp sea salt

1 tsp pepper

Combine all ingredients in a medium sauce pan over medium high heat. Bring to a boil and lower heat to medium low. Simmer for 45 min to 1 hour. Watch the water level. If the soup starts to become too thick, add ½ cup more water. Lentils and vegetables should be tender. Makes 4-6 servings.

Kathy Parry

Sides

Asparagus with Leeks and Sugar Snap Peas

Jicama Mango Slaw

Quinoa with Roasted Vegetables and Capers

Peas, Vidalia Onions and Mushrooms

Asparagus with Leeks and Sugar Snap Peas

Nothing is more appealing in the spring than a lovely side of green! And what better combination than these three. The leeks cook into a sweeter version of an onion, complementing the asparagus and snap peas. If you don't have lemon olive oil add a bit of extra lemon zest.

2 TBS olive oil

2 leeks, sliced in half and then chopped into semi-circles

1 bunch of asparagus – woody bottoms snapped off and sliced into 1/3s

2 cups sugar snap peas

1 TBS lemon flavored olive oil

1 tsp. lemon zest

Salt and pepper to taste

In a medium sauté pan, heat the olive oil over medium heat. Add the leeks and sauté for about 10 minutes until soft and sweet. Add the asparagus, and sauté another five minutes. Finally add the sugar snap peas. Stir for about another five minutes until all vegetables are tender. Drizzle the lemon oil over all the pan and sprinkle the lemon zest. Salt and pepper to taste. Serves 4-6

Note: A microplane is the best kitchen tool to use for zesting citrus fruit. They are available at all kitchen stores. Stop zesting when you reach the white portion of the peel because this is bitter.

Jicama Mango Slaw

This is the perfect side for fish tacos, grilled chicken or even the Quinoa Black Bean Soup found under spring soups! Cabbage and broccoli both fall into the cruciferous family of vegetables and are known for their cancer fighting properties and high fiber content.

1 jalapeno, chopped (wear plastic gloves!)

4 cups jicama cut into julienned strips

12 oz cut cabbage or broccoli slaw mix (about 4 cups)

½ cup chopped cilantro

3 green onions, chopped

Juice of 2 limes

1 fresh mango, chopped (about 2 cups)

1 tsp. sea salt

1 tsp. cumin

1 tsp. black pepper

Combine all the ingredients in a large bowl. Allow to sit at least 30 minutes before serving to let the flavors develop. This is a salad that tastes even better the next day as the flavors have time to fully marry. Serves 6-8.

Quinoa with Roasted Vegetables and Capers

I made this on a cold spring day when the only sign of life in my herb garden were a few sprigs of thyme. The acid in the olives and capers offsets the earthiness of the mushrooms and cauliflower. For non-vegetarians add a fried egg or piece of grilled salmon to the top. It was so tasty I ate a ridiculously large portion!

1 cup quinoa cooked according to package directions

2 cups broccoli cut in bite sized pieces

2 cups cauliflower cut in bit sized pieces

½ onion, chopped

1 ½ cups shitake mushrooms, quartered

2 TBS coconut oil

½ tsp. garlic powder

½ tsp. dried thyme

Salt and pepper to taste

½ cup pitted Kalamata olives, roughly chopped

¼ cup capers, drained

1/3 cup pine nuts

2 tsp. fresh thyme, chopped

Cook the quinoa according to package directions. It should yield close to 2 cups. Preheat the oven to 400 degrees. Put the coconut oil on a baking sheet with sides. Place it in the oven for about a minute to heat/melt the coconut oil. Remove from oven and add the broccoli, cauliflower, onion and mushrooms to the baking sheet. Sprinkle with garlic powder, dried thyme, salt and pepper. Roast the vegetables for ten minutes and stir. Roast for an additional ten minutes, stirring again after five. Roast until the vegetables are tender and a bit brown on edges. Remove from oven and toss vegetables with the quinoa in a large bowl. Add the olives, capers, pine nuts and fresh thyme. Stir to combine. Adjust seasoning with salt and pepper as needed. Serves 4-6 as a side dish.

Peas, Vidalia Onions and Mushrooms

I love seeing the fresh peas return to markets at the beginning of spring. And I'm always looking for ways to use sweet Vidalia onions when they come into season. Onions and mushrooms are both great immunity boosting foods. Perfect for spring when many of us find ourselves worn out from winter!

2 TBS butter

1 large Vidalia or other sweet onion, slice in ½ and then sliced in half circles

10 oz. baby portabella or cremi mushrooms, sliced, about 2 cups

10 oz. fresh peas, about 1 ½ cups

1 tsp dried tarragon or 1 TBS fresh, chopped

Sea salt to taste

In a large sauté pan heat the butter over medium high heat. Add the onions after the butter has melted. Sauté the onions for 8-10 minutes or until soft and translucent. Add the mushrooms, peas, tarragon and salt. Stir over heat for 2 minutes. Cover and let veggies simmer for 2-4 minutes. Don't overcook the peas as they will get hard. Serves 4 -6

Entrees

Cannellini Beans with Kale and Fried Eggs

Wild Mushroom, Thyme and Walnut Patties
with Caramelized Purple Onions

Kale and Rice Stuffed Poblano Peppers
with Chipotle Tomato Sauce

Cauliflower Crusted Vegetable Shepherd's Pie

Cannellini Beans with Kale and Fried Eggs

These are wonderful on top of the Mushroom Walnut Patties. They add sweetness and depth. AnI am a huge fan of beans and greens. As a vegetarian heading into an Italian restaurant it is often what I look for on the menu. This version cooks up quickly and is hardy for a cool spring evening. Try to only use the San Marzano tomatoes. They add a sweetness that is wonderful with beans.

1 TBS olive oil

3 cloves garlic, minced

½ cup diced yellow onion

1 15oz can organic cannellini or great northern beans

1 cup canned San Marzano tomatoes, crushed

6 cups of greens like Tuscan kale or spinach

½ cup vegetable or chicken broth

¼ cup red wine

½ tsp sea salt

1 tsp dried Italian herbs

1 TBS balsamic vinegar

½ tsp red pepper flakes (optional)

Heat the olive oil over medium heat in a large skillet. Add the garlic and onion and sauté for 2-3 minutes, careful not to burn. Rinse the beans with water and add to the pan. Add the tomatoes, broth, kale and red wine and cook over medium to medium/low heat for five minutes stirring. Stir in the salt, herbs and vinegar and optional red pepper flakes and cook for another 10 minutes until kale is soft and flavors are combined. A fried egg is an option on top that I really enjoy. While the beans and greens are cooking fry 2-4 eggs in another skillet. Portion the beans into 2-4 bowls, depending on if it is a main dish or a side. Top the beans with the fried egg. Serves 2 as a main course and 4 as a side.

Wild Mushroom, Thyme and Walnut Patties with Caramelized Purple Onions

Thyme is the first herb I can harvest from my herb garden in the early spring. The mushrooms make these patties earthy and hearty. I like the baby portabellas and shiitake mushrooms together. I can't quite call them burgers because they are better not on a bun. They are a bit moister than some vegetarian patties. Make sure your pan is very hot when you go to sear them. Getting them brown quickly will help them hold together. Serve them with the caramelized onions (recipe on right page) and a bit of Dijon.

½ purple onion, rough chopped

1 large carrot, rough chopped

12-14 oz mixed fresh mushrooms or about 5 cups, cleaned

2 cloves garlic

1 cup walnuts

½ tsp. garlic powder

½ tsp. onion powder

½ tsp. sea salt

½ tsp. black pepper

1 TBS fresh thyme (or 1 tsp. dried)

2 TBS olive oil - divided

In the bowl of a food processor add the onion and carrot. Pulse for 3 or 4 pulses. Add the mushrooms, garlic and walnuts and process until smooth. Add the garlic powder, onion powder, salt, pepper and thyme. Scrape the bowl of the food processor down if needed. Your mixture should be moist but dense enough to hold together. Put 1 TBS of olive oil in a non-stick skillet or cast iron pan over medium heat. Pour the entire mixture into the skillet and cook stirring for 10 minutes. Don't allow the mixture to stick. This step is important so the liquid from the vegetables is released. Transfer the mixture to a bowl and chill for at least an hour and even as long as overnight. (You can speed this up by putting it in the freezer for about 30 minutes.)

Remove the mixture from the refrigerator and form into four large patties. Heat another 1 TBS of olive oil in a medium skillet. If your skillet is non-stick it is still important to use some oil for flavor and browning. A cast iron pan works well for these. Cook patties on first side until brown. Flip the patties and cook again until brown and heated through. If you like a little cheese this would be the time to add a mild cheese like Havarti or Muenster to the patties. Cover the pan and turn on low to melt cheese. Remove from heat, top with caramelized purple onions (recipe below) and Dijon mustard. Serves 4.

Caramelized Purple Onions

These are wonderful on top of the Mushroom Walnut Patties. They add sweetness and depth. And yes...go on and embrace the butter.

1 large purple onion, sliced into rings

2 TBS butter

Salt to taste

Over medium heat, melt the butter in a skillet. Add the onions and sauté, stirring occasionally for 10 minutes. Turn the heat down to low and put a cover on the pan. Cook on low for another 15 minutes or until the onions are very wilted and sweet to taste. Salt to taste.

Kale and Rice Stuffed Poblano Peppers with Chipotle Tomato Sauce

With Cinco de Mayo at the beginning of May, what better time to get cooking with a little Mexican attitude? I adore stuffing Poblanos. They aren't too spicy themselves...but the jalapeno in the filling does add a bit of kick. Of course you can also make these with green peppers for a milder version. And if you don't do dairy, omit the queso fresco and add some black beans instead.

Filling

1 TBS olive oil

1 cup of chopped onions

6 cups baby kale (5 oz bag)

1 jalapeno pepper diced fine (where plastic gloves to chop)

12 oz queso fresco (buy it with Mexican cheeses)

2 cups cooked brown rice or quinoa

1 tsp ground cumin

Salt and pepper to taste

Sauce

15 oz can organic tomato sauce

1 single canned chipotle pepper in adobe sauce

1 tsp chili powder

1 tsp cumin

½ tsp salt

½ tsp garlic powder

3 large poblano peppers sliced in half lengthwise with seeds and ribs removed

For filling:

Preheat oven to 350 degrees.

In a large skillet, heat the olive oil over medium heat and add the chopped onion. Sauté for 5 minutes. Add the baby kale and jalapeno. Sauté until the kale is wilted. Remove from heat. Add the rice to the pan and crumble the queso cheese over the rice. Sprinkle the cumin, salt and pepper over everything and mix very well to combine. Set aside.

To make the sauce:

Put the chipotle pepper into the bowl of a food processor. Pulse and process until smooth. Add the tomato sauce, chili powder, cumin, salt and garlic powder.

To assemble:

Spread about a quarter of the sauce across the bottom of a rectangular baking dish, approximately 7 x 11. Place the pepper halves on top of the sauce. Fill each pepper very full with the stuffing. If you have left over stuffing just put it on the sides of the peppers. Spoon the rest of the sauce over the peppers. Cover the pan with foil and put in prepared oven for 45-50 minutes. Serves 4-6. (A half a pepper is generally a serving but I've seen my teens eat 2)

Cauliflower Crusted Vegetable Shepherd's Pie

When I developed this recipe I simple wrote the word YUM next to my notes after tasting it. And bonus – I served it to my 16 year old and he ate it without complaint. Even told me it was pretty good. Leeks scream spring to me and this dish is perfect for a chilly March or April dinner. It can be served with a salad or a protein but stands alone well as a vegetarian entrée.

Topping

6 cups chopped cauliflower

1/3 cup plain non-fat yogurt or Greek yogurt

2 TBS butter

½ tsp sea salt

1/3 cup shredded cheese

Filling

2 TBS butter

2 leeks, washed and sliced

2 large carrots sliced

1 cup broccoli florets

1 cup cauliflower florets

1 cup frozen peas

3 TBS flour of choice (I used coconut flour)

1 cup vegetable broth

½ tsp sea salt

½ tsp dried thyme

½ tsp black pepper

½ tsp garlic powder

For Topping:

Over medium high heat, steam the cauliflower in a steaming basket set into large sauce pan for approximately 10 minutes or until soft. Transfer the cauliflower to the bowl of a food processor. Add the butter and pulse for ten seconds. Add the yogurt, salt and cheese. Pulse until smooth. Set aside.

For Filling:

Melt the butter in a large skillet set over medium heat. Add the leeks and sauté for 5-7 minutes until quite soft. Add the carrots, broccoli, cauliflower and peas. Sauté, stirring for five minutes. Sprinkle flour over vegetable mixture and stir well for 2 minutes. Add the broth and bring to a simmer. Add the salt, thyme, pepper and garlic powder. Simmer for 5 minutes.

To Assemble:

Transfer the vegetable filling to a medium-sized glass or ceramic baking dish (something not quite as big as 9 x 13) Top the entire casserole with the cauliflower mixture. Smooth the mixture over the top. Put the dish into the preheated oven. Bake for 30-40 minutes uncovered and just until top barely begins to show some light browning. Serves 6-8

Chapter 3

Summer

Bounty and abundance fill summer plates at cookouts, graduation parties and picnics. We crave the al fresco eating experience. A setting sun with a group of friends outside is a dining practice most of us don't get year round, so it's best to take advantage of both the foods and setting of summer. Visit a farmers market. Talk to your farmer. Try something new. Pick something off a vine. Get to know your food source in the summer. Bring home the bounty of a garden or grow your own. And then get it on the plate with these full-flavor summer recipes.

Beginnings and Apps

Fresh Tomato Lime Salsa

Caponata

Kale Hummus

Guacamole with Mangos

Fresh Tomato Lime Salsa

Forget the jarred stuff, salsa is really simple to make. And fresh salsa has all the benefits of raw food unlike the cooked stuff in a jar. The lime in this salsa makes it super refreshing. And remember you don't always have to dip fried chips into it! Look for baked chips or chips with added nutrients like flax or quinoa. Or use cucumber slices or red peppers for dipping!

4 cups fresh tomatoes any variety

1 red pepper, chopped in chunks

½ cucumber, chopped in chunks

1 fresh jalapeno (use gloves to chop) or ¼ cup pickled jalapenos

1 cup cilantro leaves – loosely packed

1, 4 oz can green chilies

Juice of 1 lime

1 tsp. ground cumin

½ tsp. sea salt

Quarter the tomatoes and rough chop the red pepper, cucumber and jalapeno. Put all of them into a food processor and pulse a couple of times. Add the cilantro, chilies, lime, cumin and salt. Pulse until desired consistency. Letting the salsa chill for a couple hours helps intensify the flavors. Adjust the heat with more or less jalapeno. Makes 4 cups.

Caponata

Known as an Italian relish, caponata uses the bounty of a summer to compliment many dishes. Use it as an appetizer served in small bowls, stir it into eggs, dollop it on a protein or top a sandwich with it. It is so versatile and tasty. I prefer to eat it by the spoonful myself!

3 TBS olive oil

1 medium eggplant, diced in ½ inch cubes

1 medium onion, diced

4 cloves of garlic, minced

2 ribs of celery, diced

3 large tomatoes, diced

3 TBS red wine vinegar

2 TBS capers

1/3 cup chopped basil

½ tsp. sea salt

½ tsp. pepper, ground fresh

In a large sauté pan with sides heat the olive oil over medium to medium high heat. Add the eggplant, onion and garlic and cook for 5 minutes. The eggplant absorbs the olive oil quickly, so keep stirring. Add the celery, tomatoes and vinegar. Cook for 10 minutes stirring occasionally. Add the capers, basil, salt and pepper. Cover and simmer another 10-15 minutes or until vegetables are quite soft and some of the eggplant has lost its cube shape. Cool caponata and serve at room temperature. This is dish that often tastes better the next day. Make approximately 3 cups.

Kale Hummus

I've seen garlic hummus, spicy hummus, horseradish hummus, cilantro hummus....BUT why hasn't anyone combine KALE, the SUPERFOOD with our favorite snack? Well, I just had to do it. Looking for a power snack that will keep you feeling full and pack a nutrient punch? Then you have to try it! But DON'T skip the sun dried tomatoes. They add a bit of sweetness that offsets the kale. You must use a food processor or a very powerful blender like a Vita-Mix to make this recipe.

4 cups roughly torn kale leaves

1 clove of garlic (2 if you're not kissing anyone soon)

1 15 oz can organic garbanzo beans, rinsed

1/3 cup tahini

juice of one lemon

1/4 cup extra virgin olive oil

1/4 cup water

1/2 tsp sea salt

1/2 tsp pepper

1/2 cup oil packed sun dried tomatoes

Place the kale leaves in the bowl of a food processor or blender with the garlic and pulse for 30 seconds. Add the garbanzo beans and process until finely chopped. Add the tahini, lemon juice, olive oil. Process until fairly smooth. Add the water, salt, and pepper. Process until desired consistency. Add the sun dried tomatoes and process until they are mostly chopped. Adjust consistency with additional water or olive oil. Serve with fresh vegetables like cucumbers, peppers and carrots. Makes about 3 cups.

Guacamole with Mangos

Trendy taco trucks and Mexican fusion restaurants are popping up everywhere. And so are designer guacamoles. Even though I've experimented with a number of combinations. Guac with mangos remains one of my favorite. These are both two of my favorite super foods. Avocados are packed with nutrients and healthy fats including one called glutathione, known as the "mother of antioxidants". This substance helps convert food to energy at the cellular level. Eat this guacamole with no guilt! And to see the easiest way to easily remove the mango from the skin and big center pit, check out my YouTube Channel.

2 ripe avocados

1 ripe mango, chopped into small pieces

1 green onion, chopped fine

Juice from ½ lemon

Sea salt to taste

Remove the avocado from the peel and discard the pit. Put the avocado in a medium bowl. Using a potato masher or large fork, mash the avocado until smooth with some chunks. Add the mango, green onion, lemon juice and salt. Stir to combine. Makes about 2 cups.

Beverages

Watermelon Mint Water

Honeydew Lime Water

Peach Mango Carrot Skin-tastic Smoothie

Red White and Blue Smoothie

Watermelon Mint Water

If you have a few left over watermelon slices after a picnic, this is the perfect way to use them instead of wrapping them up. And mint is always a refreshing addition to a cool summer drink.

4 cups water

1-2 cups watermelon chunks

½ cup mint leaves, roughly torn

Put the water in a pitcher and add the watermelon chunks and mint. Let the flavors develop in the fridge overnight. Enjoy the next day over ice. Makes 4 cups.

Honeydew Lime Water

You'll think you're at a spa after drinking this delightful flavored water in the heat of summer.

4 cups water

2 cups honeydew melon chunks

1 lime sliced

Put the water in a pitcher and add the honeydew and lime. Let the flavors develop in the fridge overnight. Enjoy the next day over ice. Makes 4 cups.

Peach Mango Carrot
Skin-tastic Smoothie

Peaches, mangos and carrots are all high in Vitamin A. And Vitamin A is crucial for great skin health. Every summer I look forward to the wonderful local peaches grown very close to my home. They add so much flavor to a smoothie! And powerful blenders like a Vita-Mix will be able to take care of the carrot with no problem.

½ banana

½ cup pineapple

½ fresh peach

½ cup mango (fresh or frozen)

½ carrot

½ cup ice cubes

Combine all ingredients in a powerful blender. Serves one.

Red, White, and Blue Smoothie

When I was in college my roommate Dianne lived in Washington, DC for the summer. She told me about the bars that made red, white and blue daiquiris for the 4th of July. Not nearly as healthy as this summer smoothie I'm sure! Use the bounty of the summer harvest to enjoy this phyto-nutrient, anti-oxidant filled smoothie.

½ banana

½ cup pineapple

½ cup blueberries

½ cup raspberries

1 TBS ground flax seed

½ cup ice cubes (if not using frozen fruit)

Combine all ingredients in a powerful blender. Serves one.

Salads

Coconut Lime Quinoa Salad with Mangos

Tomato Salad with Creamy Basil Dressing

Summer Quinoa Salad with Zucchini and Tomatoes

Marinated Green Bean Salad

Mixed Baby Greens with Blackberries

Coconut Lime Quinoa Salad
with Mangos

This dressing is so good I could drink it! After my first go around it didn't taste coconutty enough. Then, "Bam!" coconut oil. And perfection. Superfoods in this wonderful salad include: coconut oil, mangos, quinoa and onions. I buy the roasted coconut chips at Trader Joes, but many natural food stores carry them.

Salad:

Cook one cup of quinoa per package directions. This should yield approximately 2 cups.

1 cup celery, chopped

1 cup fresh or frozen mango chopped

¼ cup finely chopped red onion

2 carrots, peeled and sliced on the diagonal

½ cup roasted coconut chips unsweetened

Coconut Lime Dressing

1 cup light coconut milk

Juice of one lime

1 tsp. lime zest

1" fresh ginger, peeled and sliced

3 TBS. coconut oil

½ tsp. salt

3-4 pickled jalapeno slices

Cool the quinoa in bowl in the refrigerator. Add the remaining ingredients except coconut chips and mix together. Add approximately 2/3 of a cup of the Coconut Lime Dressing. Toss to combine. Add more dressing if desired. Salt and pepper the salad to taste. Sprinkle coconut chips on top. Serves 4-6

Combine all ingredients in the pitcher of a heavy duty blender. Blend on high power for 30 seconds. Transfer to a jar and save extra dressing, refrigerated for up to two weeks.

NOTE: If you like more heat, you can add additional jalapenos, chilis or red pepper flakes

Tomato Salad with Creamy Basil Dressing

The bounty of the harvest this time of year always leaves me scrambling for tomato, basil and zucchini recipes! Here is a simple combo great for lunch or served as a side at dinner. And you will want to use this dressing all summer long!

4 tomatoes, chopped into 1 inch pieces

1 15 oz can organic chick peas, drained and rinsed

1 cup shredded zucchini

2 cup kale or spinach chopped

Creamy Basil Dressing

1 cup basil leaves

¼ cup plain organic Greek yogurt

2 Tbs. organic mayonnaise

1 TBS olive oil

1 TBS balsamic vinegar

1 clove minced garlic

Salt and pepper to taste

For salad:

Combine all ingredients in a small bowl. Pour dressing over the salad. Gently combine and season with salt and pepper as needed. Serves 2-4.

For Dressing:

In a blender combine all ingredients. Blend for 10-20 seconds until well combined. Season with salt and pepper after all other ingredients have been blended.

Summer Quinoa Salad with Zucchini and Tomatoes

Quinoa is the nutty grain from South America that cooks quickly and is full of nutrients and protein. Use it as a base for these classic summer combination.

1 cup quinoa, cooked according to package and cooled

NOTE: This should yield 2+ cups cooked.

1 cup chopped fresh basil

1 clove garlic chopped

2 cups diced tomatoes or cherry tomatoes, cut in half

1 cup shredded zucchini

1 cup fennel bulb chopped fine

½ cup olive oil

Juice of one lemon

½ cup feta (optional)

½ tsp. sea salt (or to taste)

pepper to taste

Cook the quinoa according to the package and cool. Add the basil, garlic, tomatoes, zucchini and fennel to the quinoa. Toss until well combined. Drizzle the olive oil over the salad and add lemon juice. Toss well. Add feta and salt and pepper to taste. Serves 4 – 6.

Marinated Green Bean Salad

I fell in love with marinated vegetable salads when I was in high school. Back then we dumped a big bottle of Italian Style dressing over veggies and called it done. Now I know better than to trust the ingredients in most big-brand salad dressings. Usually they are filled with some type of MSG and preservatives. This is simple and uses real ingredients.

1 lb green beans, cut into 2" pieces

1 cup cherry tomatoes, sliced in half

½ cup chopped basil

1 15 oz can organic chick peas, drained

½ cup extra virgin olive oil

5 TBS red wine vinegar

2 cloves chopped garlic

½ tsp sea salt

½ tsp black pepper

Steam the green beans until tender. Remove from the heat and quickly run under cold water to halt the cooking process. Combine the green beans with all the other ingredients in a large bowl. Allow to marinate for at least an hour in the refrigerator and as long as overnight. Stir occasionally if leaving for a long period.

Serves 6-8

Mixed Baby Greens
with Blackberries

It is very hard for me to make recipes with berries because I just eat them...unadorned. But one of my favorite uses for berries is in a mixed salad. We tend to think of berries for desserts and breakfast foods, but they are wonderful paired with a green like arugula or other baby greens with some bite. If you can't find a fig vinegar, use another fruit-based vinegar or just a plain balsamic.

2 cups blackberries, black raspberries and/or red raspberries

½ cup chopped walnuts

1 green onion sliced thin

6 cups mixed baby greens or arugula

Fig Vinaigrette:

½ cup extra virgin olive oil

4 TBS fig vinegar (or balsamic)

½ tsp. Dijon mustard

1 TBS honey

Pinch of sea salt

Combine all salad ingredients in a large bowl. Shake all the ingredients for the dressing in a glass jar with a lid. Toss dressing with greens to combine. Serves 4-6.

Soups

Golden Beet and Yellow Pepper Soup

Asian Gazpacho

Golden Beet and Yellow Pepper Soup

Cold beet soup sounds a little odd if you've never had it. But when the yellow beets start popping up at farmers markets in late summer, I get a craving for this delicious golden soup. When I served it to my family no one even knew what vegetable it was. But they all thought it was delicious. Delicate and sweet. Beets are high in natural sugars, so I keep the skins on to add fiber. [Picture on page 92.]

3 TBS olive oil

5 large gold beets (6-8 small)

2 yellow peppers

1 medium sweet onion, chopped

Salt and pepper

2 cups vegetable broth

Preheat oven to 425. Put the olive oil on a baking sheet with sides. Leave the skin on the beets, trim the stems down to ¼ inch and slice them in half or quarters (about 1-2 inch pieces), depending on the size. Rough chop the yellow peppers into 1 inch pieces. Put the beets, peppers and onions on the prepared baking sheet. Sprinkle the vegetables with salt and pepper. Roast the vegetables for 10 minutes, open the oven and stir with a metal spatula. Roast for another 10-15 minutes or until veggies are browning and beets are tender. Allow the vegetables to cool for 10 minutes and transfer to a powerful blender. Pour 2 cups of vegetable broth over the vegetables and blend on high for about 2 minutes. Transfer to a glass container and chill for at least 2 hours or overnight. (Side note...this is also good warm!) Serves 4-6.

Asian Gazpacho

Everyone knows the cold Mexican soup. But adding an Asian twist to this classic really surprises your palette...in a fun way. And the bonus of this soup is you get RAW veggies. Raw vegetables have the most nutrients but it's often hard to eat enough of them. A food processor and not a blender is best for the texture of this soup.

4 cups tomatoes

1 medium cucumber

1 red pepper

2 stalks celery

4 green onions

½ cup parsley

½ cup cilantro

1 TBS grated fresh ginger

1 clove garlic, minced

¼ cup rice wine vinegar

¼ cup soy sauce

½ tsp sea salt

½ tsp pepper

½ tsp red pepper flakes (optional)

Sriracha sauce for garnish

Rough chop the tomatoes, cucumber, red pepper, celery and green onions. Place them all in the bowl of a food processor along with the parsley, cilantro, ginger and garlic. Pulse 4-5 times until well broken up and minced well. Add the rice wine vinegar, soy sauce and salt and pepper (and optional red pepper flakes). Pulse quickly to combine. Transfer soup to large bowl. Chill for 30 minutes. Serve with a garnish of Sriracha sauce if you like heat. Serves 4-6.

Sides

Swiss Chard with Olives and Roasted Red Peppers

Bok Choy with Coconut Oil and Turmeric

Seeded Yellow Squash Bake

Green Beans with Lemon Garlic Thyme and Walnuts

Swiss Chard with Olives and Roasted Red Peppers

As a child I did not like Swiss Chard. I tried to feed it to the dog under the table. But my father grew big gorgeous leaves of the stuff so I eventually learned to like it. And now I love the beautifully colored stalks. When you see the rainbow chards, yellow, orange and red stalks, you know they contain a bunch of antioxidants and nutrients. A "bunch" of chard will vary by store or farmer, but you should end up with about 8 cups, chopped.

1 large bunch of Swiss chard, chopped in 2" pieces (about 8 cups)

2 TBS olive oil

2 cloves garlic, minced

1 cup sweet cherry tomatoes, sliced in half

½ cup Kalamata olives, chopped

½ cup chopped roasted red peppers

2 tsp. balsamic vinegar

¼ parmesan cheese

Salt and pepper to taste

In a medium sauté pan, heat the olive oil over medium heat. Add the garlic and tomatoes. Sauté until the tomatoes begin to soften about 5 minutes. Add the Swiss chard and cook until wilted about 3- 4 minutes. Add the olives, red peppers and cook an additions 2-3 minutes, stirring. Remove from heat. Stir in vinegar and parmesan. Season with salt and pepper to taste. Serves 4-6.

Kathy Parry

Bok Choy with Coconut Oil and Turmeric

Bok Choy is an often overlooked member of the cruciferous vegetable family (what with kale and Brussel sprouts getting all the attention!) But this cabbage-family green is loaded with nutrients, even Omega-3 fats. Coconut oil is one of the heathiest oils you can eat and turmeric is ranked high for its cancer-fighting properties.

3 baby bok choy or 1 large

2 TBS coconut oil

½ tsp smoked paprika

½ tsp turmeric

Sea salt

Cut the baby bok choy in half. If using a large bok choy, cut it into 1/8s. Be careful that each section has a part of the core so it holds together. Combine the smoked paprika and turmeric in a small bowl. Heat a skillet (preferably cast iron) over high/medium high heat. Add 1 TBS coconut oil and keep on heat until the oil is quite hot. Add 3-4 bok choy sections to the pan. While bok choy is cooking sprinkle each section with the combination of paprika and turmeric. Then sprinkle with sea salt. Allow bok choy to cook on one side for 3 minutes or until tops are beginning to wilt, then crisp. Using tongs, quickly flip the bok choy over. Repeat the sprinkling with the spices and salt. Cook another 2-3 minutes. Remove from the pan and cook a second batch. Add more coconut oil if necessary. Serves 3-4.

Seeded Yellow Squash Bake

After college I lived in North Carolina for a couple years. My southern roommates loved to make a big casserole of yellow squash. The only problem, it was filled with mayonnaise and bread crumbs...not the most energy producing foods. This is my rendition of a yellow squash bake. It is full of seeds including chia and hemp seeds that give you added protein and healthy omega 3 fats. If your garden is over-flowing with zucchini you can use it as well.

5 cups yellow summer squash, sliced in rounds

2 TBS butter

1 cup chopped onion

1/3 cup hemp seeds

¼ cup chia seeds

½ cup plain Greek yogurt

2 eggs

1 tsp. garlic powder

1 tsp. sea salt

1 tsp. black pepper

½ cup raw, unsalted sunflower seeds

Preheat oven to 350 degrees. In a medium skillet over medium high heat, sauté the squash in the butter with the onions for about 5-8 minutes. Remove from the heat. And transfer to a large mixing bowl. Add the hemp and chia seeds. In another small bowl combine the yogurt and eggs. Whisk to combine. Stir the garlic powder, salt, and pepper into the yogurt mixture. Pour this liquid mixture over the squash and gently combine. Coat a 6 x 9 (or equivalent) ceramic or glass baking dish with non-stick cooking spray. Pour squash mixture into the pan. Top with the ½ cup of sunflower seeds. Cover the dish with foil and bake for 30 minutes. Remove and cut into squares. Serves 6

Green Beans with Lemon Garlic Thyme and Walnuts

When I was a child, I was not allowed to go swimming until I picked several rows of beans from my father's organic garden. At the end of the day, exhausted from my swim, I was then parked in front of the TV while I snapped the grocery bag full of beans. Later my mother froze them for winter. And even though those beans were the bane of my childhood summers, I loved to eat them! I still do, but I like them jazzed up a bit. Thyme is plentiful all summer long and adding nuts to any vegetable dish raises the protein profile.

1 lb organic green beans, washed and trimmed

2 TBS olive oil

2 cloves garlic minced

Juice from ½ lemon

¼ cup water

2 tsp. lemon zest

1 TBS chopped fresh thyme

¼ cup chopped walnuts

Sea salt

Place a skillet over medium high heat. Heat the olive oil and add the garlic. Stir for about a minute. Add the green beans and lemon juice. Stir and cook for about 5 minutes. Add the water if the pan is becoming dry. Cover and simmer for about 3 minutes or until beans are tender. Add the lemon zest, thyme and walnuts. Season with sea salt. Serves 4-6

Note: Use a microplane to zest the lemon. These are sold in all kitchen stores. An alternative to adding lemon zest is to add a few drops of lemon essential oil. If you don't know about these wonderful oils, you can learn more on my website. www.kathyparry.com

Entrees

Chickpea Burgers with Cilantro Tahini Yogurt Sauce

Roasted Summer Vegetable Lasagna with Pesto Filling

Savory Zucchini Crusted Mexican Tart

Soba Noodle with Peanut Thai Sauce

Chickpea Burgers with Cilantro Tahini Yogurt Sauce

A little bit falafel inspired but not deep fried and filled with more nutrients! Yum. Top with a big old fresh-from-the-garden tomato. The hemp seeds are filled with healthy omega-3s and are moist enough to help keep the patties together without the addition of eggs or filler.

2, 15 oz cans organic chick peas, rinsed and drained

½ cup shelled hemp seed

½ cup raw sunflower seeds

½ cup cilantro

½ cup parsley

2 tsp cumin

1 tsp coriander

1 tsp garlic powder

1 tsp sea salt

1 tsp pepper

2-4 TBS olive oil for frying

Cilantro Tahini Yogurt Sauce

1/3 cup tahini

1 cup fresh cilantro

1 clove fresh garlic

1 cup plain Greek yogurt

Juice of 1 lemon

½ tsp salt

Add all the ingredients to the bowl of a food processor. Pulse until ingredients are chopped and beginning to clump together. Transfer to a wide bowl. Mix by hand with a spatula and combine well. Form mixture into 6 patties. The mixture should be moist and hold together well. If for some reason it is too dry or too moist, correct with a bit of water or hemp seed. Set aside and make the Cilantro Tahini Yogurt Sauce.

Combine all the ingredients in a powerful blender. Blend until smooth. Makes 1 cup. Set aside until burgers are cooked.

Cooking and Assembly

Frying pan method: Heat 2 TBS of the olive oil in a frying pan over medium high heat. Form the chick pea mixture into 6 patties. Add 2-3 of the patties at a time to the pan. Cook until slightly brown on each side. Transfer to plates. Heat the remaining oil and fry the rest of the patties.

Oven method: Heat oven to 450 and patties placed on a baking sheet that has been coated with non-stick cooking spray. Bake 5-7 minutes. Open oven, remove tray and flip the patties. Bake another 5-7 minutes.

Serve the burgers with a slice of fresh tomato and a big dollop of the Cilantro Tahini Yogurt Sauce. Serves 6.

Roasted Summer Vegetable Lasagna with Pesto Filling

This may be a little more time consuming to produce than some recipes in this book, but SO worth it. I set out to prove that you can make a delicious lasagna without the noodles. It is best to make this a day ahead. When the lasagna has time to sit, the flavors increase and the liquid from the vegetables absorbs. [Picture on page 222.]

1 eggplant

1 large zucchini or 2 small 6-7 inch

3 large portabella mushrooms

1 ½ cup pesto (see besto-pesto below)

2 cups tomato sauce (see below)

1 cup ricotta cheese

1 egg

½ cup grated parmesan

8 sliced fresh mozzarella

My All-Purpose Tomato Sauce

15 oz can organic diced tomatoes

15 oz can organic tomato sauce

2 TBS tomato paste

1 tsp garlic powder

2 tsp dried Italian herb blend

Combine all ingredients in a small bowl. Set aside.

Vegetables:

Preheat oven to 425 degrees. Spray two baking sheets with non-stick olive oil spray. Slice the eggplant and zucchini lengthwise in 1/8 inch thick slices. Slice each of the mushrooms in 1/8 inch thick slices as well. Lay the eggplant slices on one baking sheet and sprinkle with salt and garlic powder. On the other sheet place the zucchini and mushrooms. Put the cookie sheets in the preheated oven. Bake for five minutes and then flip the eggplant over. Put the eggplant back in the oven bake all veggies another 5-8 minutes. It is important to let the mushrooms and zucchini release their liquid so your lasagna isn't too runny.

Assembly:

Preheat the oven to 350 degrees. In a small bowl combine the ricotta, egg and ¼ cup shredded parmesan. Make the tomato sauce and set aside. Make the pesto and set aside.

[Continued on next page]

Put ½ cup of the tomato sauce in the bottom of an 8 x 10 baking pan. Layer the eggplant slices on top of the sauce. Spread the ricotta mixture over the eggplant slices. Top with a few spoonfuls of tomato sauce. Layer the mushrooms on top of the ricotta/sauce layer. Top the mushroom layer with 1 ½ cups of pesto. Top the pesto with the zucchini. Spread about ¾ cup of sauce on top of the zucchini. Top the sauce with slices of fresh mozzarella and the remaining ¼ cup parmesan. Bake the lasagna for 40 minutes. The lasagna MUST sit for at least 30 minutes before slicing. If you skip this step the lasagna will be very runny. It is actually best served at room temperature or refrigerate and serve the next day. Makes 6-8 servings.

It has taken me a few years to actually remember what I do when I make pesto. Usually I make it by feel. But I was teaching my daughter to make it, and realized I better measure and record. Here is my best.

Combine the basil and garlic in a food processor. Pulse for 2-3 seconds. Add the nuts and pulse a couple times. Add the remaining ingredients and process until smooth. Add more olive oil or water to make it your favorite consistency.

Besto Pesto

4 cups basil leaves

4 cloves garlic, smashed and roughly chopped

½ cup walnuts or pinenuts

½ cup extra virgin olive oil

½ cup parmesan cheese

½ cup water

½ tsp salt

1 TBS balsamic vinegar

Savory Zucchini Crusted Mexican Tart

This is an easy pie to throw together with ingredients you probably have on hand in the summer. I'm not a big fan of jarred condiments, but sometimes it is hard to escape a little jarred salsa. Look for a good quality local or organic salsa.

Zucchini Crust

4 cups shredded zucchini (1 large or 2-3 small)

¼ cup chopped yellow onion

1 cup shredded cheddar cheese

½ tsp salt

¼ tsp cumin

¼ tsp chili powder

2 eggs

Black Bean Layer

1 15 oz can organic black beans

¼ cup jarred salsa

¼ tsp cumin

¼ tsp chili powder

2 tsp hot sauce (optional)

6 slices tomato

¼ cup shredded cheddar cheese

¼ cup good quality jarred salsa or fresh

Preheat oven to 400 degrees. In a large bowl toss the shredded zucchini, onion, cheese and seasonings. Combine well. Crack the eggs in a small bowl and scramble. Pour the eggs into the zucchini mixture and combine well. Coat a 10" glass pie plate with olive oil based cooking spray. Pour zucchini mixture into the pie plate and gently press the mixture up the sides of the plate and smooth across the bottom. Bake in the preheated oven for 20 minutes.

While the crust is baking, combine the black beans, salsa, cumin, chili powder and hot sauce in the bowl of a food processor. Process until fairly smooth, with a few chunks. Set aside.

Remove the crust from the oven and gently spread the black bean mixture over the top. Put 6 spoonfuls of salsa around the crust and top each dollop of salsa with a slice of tomato. Sprinkle the ¼ cup of shredded cheddar over the entire tart. Bake for an additional 10 minutes at 400 degrees.

Allow the tart to cool for 10 minutes and slice into 6 pieces. Serves 4-6

Soba Noodle with Peanut Thai Sauce

This sauce makes me so happy. And the use of shredded cabbage is a great way to get this much under-used veggie in your diet. It has fiber and cancer-fighting properties, but for some reason in this country we tend to think of it mostly as a coleslaw ingredient. Use only natural, unsweetened peanut butter. Look for rice based soba noodles in the Asian section of your grocery store.

2 TBS Peanut oil or sunflower oil

½ cup chopped onion

1 clove garlic chopped

1 cup carrots sliced on diagonal

½ cup red peppers

1 1/2 cups broccoli florets

3 cups shredded cabbage

½ pound soba rice noodles

½ cup organic vegetable or chicken broth

Peanut Thai Sauce

½ cup water

¼ cup tablespoons rice wine vinegar

2 green onions, rough chopped

1/3 cup natural peanut butter – no sugar

¼ cup soy sauce

1 inch piece fresh ginger

1 tablespoon dark sesame oil

Heat the oil in a sauté pan over medium high heat. Add the garlic and onion and sauté for 2-3 minutes. Add the carrots, peppers, broccoli and cabbage. Turn heat to medium and sauté, stirring the vegetables every few minutes for about 10 minutes.

While the vegetables are cooking, fill a large pot with water and bring to a boil. Boil the soba noodles according to package directions. Make sure they don't get too soft. They usually only take 5 minutes or less. Drain. Add the noodles to the vegetables in the sauté pan. Add ½ cup broth and stir over low heat. Add the peanut sauce and stir until well combined and heated through. Makes 4 servings.

In a powerful blender place all the sauce ingredients. Blend for one minute. Set aside.

Chapter 4

Fall

Cooler nights and sunny days allow the last of the heartier vegetables to stay on the vines, trees and stalks a bit longer. Apples, squash, Brussel sprouts and kale are all abundant in the fall garden. Although summer's bounty steals the produce show, I enjoy the selection of fall vegetables the best of any all year. Earthy, bold, strong flavors punctuate fall foods. And don't even get me started on the most perfect fruit ever: an apple picked directly off the tree on a September afternoon. Enjoy the complex flavors of fall in these recipes.

Beginnings and Apps

Sweet Potato Hummus

Buffalo Cauliflower with Blue Cheese Dip

Eggplant "Meatballs" with Tomato Sauce

Polenta Triangles with Sage Pesto and Goat Cheese

Lettuce Wraps with Cauliflower Fried "Rice"

Sweet Potato Hummus

I have become a huge fan of flavored hummus. Why stick with regular when you can jazz it up and make it more nutrient dense? This is wonderful served in the fall and winter. You will find sweet potatoes used pretty liberally throughout this book. And with good reason. They are a superfood, loaded with vitamins like A and C, fiber and phytonutrients.

1 medium sweet potato

1 15 oz can organic chick peas, drained and rinsed

juice from one lemon (about 1/4 cup)

1/4 cup tahini

2 TBS olive oil

1 tsp cumin

1 clove garlic, chopped

1/4 tsp sea salt

3-4 TBS water

Chop the sweet potato into 1/2 pieces, leave the skin on for more fiber and nutrients. Steam, boil or cook with a bit of water in the microwave until tender. Steaming generally takes 10 minutes, boiling 8 minutes and microwave with water about five minutes.

Drain the sweet potatoes and run cold water over them.

Transfer sweet potatoes to a food processor or blender. Add the rest of the ingredients except the water. Process for about one minute. Add water as needed to smooth. Process another 2 minutes until smooth.

Keeps in refrigerator for five days. Serves with veggies or pita. Makes 2 cups.

Buffalo Cauliflower with Blue Cheese Dip

Who says only wings can be spicy and dipped in blue cheese? I made this as an appetizer for a Friday night happy hour at my house and it was by far the most popular one on the table! Break out of the ordinary and the bottles of pre-made sauce. Adjust the smoked paprika and cayenne to adjust the heat level.

½ head of cauliflower chopped into florets

1 TBS olive oil

½ tsp onion powder

½ tsp garlic powder

½ tsp sea salt

½ tsp smoked paprika

¼ tsp cayenne pepper

Blue Cheese Dip

2/3 cup plain Greek yogurt

2 TBS organic mayonnaise

½ cup crumbled blue cheese

½ tsp sea salt

1 tsp red wine vinegar

Fresh ground black pepper

For the Cauliflower

Preheat the oven to 425 degrees. On a baking sheet with sides toss the cauliflower with the olive oil. In a small bowl combine all the seasonings. Sprinkle the seasonings over the cauliflower and toss with your hands. You may not need all the seasoning depending on your comfort level with spices. Bake the cauliflower in the prepared oven for 10 minutes then stir with a large spoon or metal spatula. Bake another 10 minutes and remove. Cool to at least room temperature before serving. Serves 6 as an appetizer.

For the Blue Cheese Dip

Combine all the ingredients in a small bowl. Put next to the cauliflower for dipping.

Eggplant "Meatballs" with Tomato Sauce

So tasty. I love it when non-vegetarians have no idea what they are eating, only that it tastes delicious. My guy launched into these and loved them. Then I revealed they were eggplant! "Well they rock!" was his response. The batter is a bit moist and they don't necessarily stay in a "ball" when you cook them. Just be gentle when you're turning them over. This can easily be a main course as well as an appetizer.

1 eggplant, cut into 1" cubes

2 TBS olive oil

1 cup organic instant oats

2 cloves garlic, minced

¼ cup chopped onion

2 tsp dried Italian herbs

1 tsp sea salt

1 tsp pepper

½ cup parmesan cheese

4 TBS olive oil for frying

Basil-Filled Tomato Sauce

1 28 oz can San Marzano tomatoes

1 tsp sea salt

½ tsp black pepper

½ cup fresh basil

1 tsp dried Italian herbs

1 tsp garlic powder

Preheat the oven to 350 degrees. Put the eggplant cubes on a baking sheet with the 2 TBS of olive oil. Roast the eggplant for 30 minutes. Allow the eggplant to cool for an hour or so before proceeding with the recipe. You can also roast the eggplant up to a day ahead of time. Drain any water from the bowl the eggplant has been in. Transfer the eggplant to the bowl of a food processor. Pulse the eggplant until it breaks down. Add the rest of the ingredients except the olive oil. Pulse until well combined, but be careful not to over process as it will turn to mush.

Heat half the olive oil in a large skillet or cast iron pan. If using a non-stick skillet, you can use less oil. Scoop about 2 TBS of eggplant mixture into your hands and form into balls. Fry each ball for about three minutes per side. Watch them carefully and transfer to a plate that is lined with paper towels. Continue cooking "meatballs" in batches. Serve the meatballs on top of a bowl of the marinara sauce. Serves 6 - 8 as appetizers. Makes about 20 balls.

Combine all the ingredients in the bowl of a food processor. Pulse until tomatoes and basil are well broken up. Transfer the sauce to a small sauce pan. Heat for 10-15 minutes. Makes 3 cups.

Polenta Triangles with Sage Pesto and Goat Cheese

These make a beautiful presentation for any party. The polenta can be made ahead and reheated. A great first course or appetizer for any fall party. Goat cheese is typically easier for most people to digest than cow's milk cheese. It adds a great tang to balance the sage. And for added goodness, the pesto has some kale...just keeping it all healthy!

Polenta:

3 cups water

1 cup polenta (corn meal)

1 tsp sea salt

1 TBS butter

3 TBS goat cheese

Sage Pesto:

½ cup fresh sage leaves

1 cup walnuts

1 cup kale

2 cloves garlic

½ cup olive oil

½ cup water

2 TBS balsamic vinegar

½ tsp. sea salt

Bring the water to a simmer in a medium pot. Stir the polenta in quickly with a whisk. Continue to stir for about 5-10 minutes or until the polenta begins to pull away from the sides of the pan. Transfer the polenta to a 9" glass pie pan that has been sprayed with non-stick cooking spray. Cut the butter into little pieces and place on top of the polenta. Spread it around as it melts. If serving the polenta soon, just cool for 10-15 minutes. Slice into 12 wedges. Top with a dollop of sage pesto and goat cheese. Serves 6-8 as an appetizer. (Polenta can be made ahead and reheated in the oven at 300 degrees for 10 minutes)

Combine the sage, walnuts, kale and garlic in a food processor. Pulse until well chopped. You may have to scrape down the sides. With the processor running, add the olive oil, water, balsamic and salt. Process until desired consistency. You may need a bit more water if you want it thinner. Makes 1 ½ cups.

Lettuce Wraps with Cauliflower Fried "Rice"

Yum! These could be a main course, but since most chain restaurants with lettuce wraps on the menu list them under apps, so did I. When I served these, no one eating them thought it wasn't fried rice. But there is NO rice in this dish. Cauliflower processed fine in a food processor before cooking turns into the consistency of rice. And all together it turns into delicious!

1 TBS coconut oil

1 TBS sesame oil

4 cups cauliflower cut into small florets

1 carrot, chopped in ¼ inch pieces

1 cup pea pods, chopped in ¼ inch pieces

1 cup broccoli, chopped in ¼ inch pieces

½ red pepper, chopped in ¼ inch pieces

½ medium onion, chopped in ¼ inch pieces

2 TBS grated fresh ginger (or 2 tsp. dried)

½ tsp sea salt

1 TBS rice wine vinegar

¼ cup soy sauce

2 TBS sesame seeds

2 eggs

1 head romaine lettuce

Process the cauliflower in a food processor until it is fine. Set aside. In a large skillet or wok heat the coconut oil and sesame oil over medium high heat. Add the processed cauliflower, carrot, pea pods, broccoli, red pepper and onion. Stir fry for about 8 minutes until tender. Add the ginger, salt, vinegar, soy sauce and sesame seeds. Cook for an additional two minutes.

Crack the two eggs into a small bowl and stir well.

Make a hole in the middle of the pan of vegetables by moving the vegetable to the sides. Pour the eggs into the center of the hole. Allow the eggs to cook for about a minute. Once they begin to cook, use a fork to scramble them. Before the eggs are completely cooked, stir everything together. Turn off the heat.

Peel and wash 6-8 romaine leaves. Dry the leaves. Fill each the stir fry mixture. Top with additional soy sauce or hot sauce. Serves 4-6

Beverages

Tea with Ginger and Wild Orange Essential Oil

Pumpkin Spice Smoothie

Strong Hair and Nail Sweet Potato Smoothie

Tea with Ginger and Wild Orange Essential Oil

I turn into a huge tea fan when the weather turns chilly. Tea drinker are fortunate because the benefits of tea, especially green tea have been well documented. Everything from brain function to antioxidants to improved metabolism have been linked to green tea. Essential oils are the most concentrated form of oil extracted from a plant. They can be used in food, atomized into the air or rubbed on the body. Many of them have amazing health benefits.

Email me (Kathy@KathyParry.com) if you want to learn more about them! If you don't have Essential Oils, you can use some orange zest. (The peel chopped very fine or zested on a microplane).

1 cup green tea	While the tea is steeping, add the ginger and orange oil or zest. You can also put the ginger and zest into a steeping ball or spoon and remove them when the tea is ready. Steep for 5 minutes.
1 tsp. chopped fresh ginger	
2 drops wild orange essential oil (or 1 tsp. zest)	
	Serves 1.

Pumpkin Spice Smoothie

Ahh, here's where you can add a bit of healthy goodness to a pumpkin spice drink! Forget the flavored lattes that have over 40 grams of sugar. Enjoy the fiber and nutrients in this smoothie instead!

½ cup canned organic pumpkin

½ cup unsweetened almond milk

½ cup frozen mango chunks

1 tsp pumpkin spice blend (on the next page)

2 TBS plain Greek yogurt

2 tsp. raw honey

2 ice cubes

Blend all ingredients on high in a blender until smooth. Serves 1.

Pumpkin Spice Blend

Spices have powerful health benefits! Cinnamon for lowering bad cholesterol and regulating blood sugar. Ginger aides digestion and decreases inflammation. Cloves help reduce upper respiratory issues and inflammation. Nutmeg helps metabolize carbohydrates and helps nutrients absorb. And all of this goodness just really tastes like fall.

5 TBS ground cinnamon

1 TBS ground ginger

1 TBS ground nutmeg

1 1/2 tsp ground cloves

Stir together and use liberally during the fall.

Strong Hair and Nail Sweet Potato Smoothie

Are you always wishing your hair and nails looked better? Stronger? Certain nutrients like biotin and Vitamin A are important for healthy hair and nails. Biotin is found in the banana, sweet potato and almonds. And mango has a very high level of Vitamin A. A sweet potato in a smoothie may sound odd, but it adds a great flavor and most powerful blenders can take care of grinding it up. Many people take a supplement for stronger hair and nails...but all you need is found in this powerful smoothie.

½ banana

½ cup mango chunks (fresh or frozen)

½ cup raw chopped sweet potato, skin on

2 TBS almond butter

3-4 ice cubes

¼ cup water to help process

Blend all ingredients on high in a blender until smooth. Serves 1.

Soups

Curried Red Lentil and Cauliflower

Black Bean Corn and Farro Soup

Italian White Bean and Tomato with Escarole

Asian Bowl with Edamame and Roasted Fall Vegetables

Curried Red Lentil and Cauliflower Soup

Wow. I ate two bowls of this after I made it – and I'm not a two-bowl-of-soup person! The list of spices may seem intimidating and if you don't have them all you could just use a tablespoon or two of curry powder. But do your cells a favor and at least go buy turmeric. The compound curcumin in the spice has been shown to have anti-cancer and anti-inflammatory properties. The soup cooks rather quickly so it is an easy meal on a hectic fall night.

2 TBS olive oil

1 cup chopped onion

3 cloves garlic, minced

1 cup red lentils (other varieties can be used but the red make it so pretty!)

3 cups chopped cauliflower

4 cups organic vegetable of chicken stock

1 28 oz can organic chopped tomatoes

1 tsp black pepper

2 tsp sea salt

1 tsp coriander

1 tsp ground ginger

½ tsp cinnamon

½ tsp cardamom

2 tsp turmeric

¼ tsp cayenne pepper (optional if you don't like it too spicy)

In a medium sauce pan, heat the olive oil over medium high heat. Add the onions and garlic and sauté for 2-3 minutes. Add the lentils and stir for another minute. Add all the remaining ingredients. Simmer for 20 – 30 minutes or until the cauliflower is tender and lentils have broken down. Serves 6.

Black Bean Corn and Farro Soup

Corn is still abundant in early fall and this soup is a wonderful way to use up leftover ears. But plain corn soup is high in sugar. Adding in all the delicious fiber from the beans and farro are a wonderful way to enjoy the flavor of corn without the sugar spikes. Farro is an ancient grain that is loaded with nutrients, although it does have a gluten profile. If trying to go without the gluten, substitute quinoa. The farro called for in this recipe is the instant variety or sometimes sold as pearlized. If you don't use instant farro, your farro will need to soak overnight and cooking time will increase by about 30 minutes.

1 medium onion, chopped

1 spicy pepper, chopped (banana pepper, Anaheim etc. omit if you don't like spice)

1 yellow bell pepper, chopped

2 ears of corn (either pre-cooked or not) kernels removed

1 28 oz can organic chopped tomatoes or 3 cups of chopped fresh tomatoes

1 15 oz can organic black beans, drained

4 cups vegetable broth

1 ½ cups water

½ cup instant farro

1 tsp cumin

1 tsp chili powder

1 tsp garlic powder

1 ½ tsp sea salt

Black pepper to taste

Add all ingredients to a medium sauce pan and simmer over medium heat for 30 – 40 minutes or until farro and vegetables are tender.

Serves 6.

Italian White Bean and Tomato with Escarole Soup

People forget about escarole. But it you haven't tried it or it has been awhile, try it in this hearty soup. Unlike kale that some people think is bitter, this green is tender and mellow. And beans are full of fiber and plant nutrients. Big win for flavor here!

1 medium onion, chopped

3 cloves garlic, minced

1 sweet red pepper, chopped

1 28 oz can chopped tomatoes

1 15 oz can cannellini or great northern beans, drained and rinsed

4 cups vegetable stock

2 cups water

6 cups chopped escarole

1 TBS dried Italian herbs

1 tsp sea salt

1 tsp black pepper

½ tsp crushed red pepper flakes (optional)

Combine all ingredients in a medium pot over medium high heat. Bring to a simmer. Simmer for 30- 40 minutes. If you like your soup a little thicker you can simmer a bit longer. Serve with a sprinkle of parmesan cheese on top. Serves 6

Asian Bowl with Edamame and Roasted Fall Vegetables

This is mostly a soup, but the components are put in a bowl and the broth is poured over at the end. The parsnips and carrots are sweet once they are roasted and are wonderful with the gingery broth. Use fresh ginger because you need this punch. And ginger and raw honey are great for digestion.

2 TBS coconut oil or olive oil

3 parsnips, peeled and cubed in ¼" pieces

3 carrots, peeled and cubed in ¼" pieces

1 cup chopped onions

2 cups cooked barley or rice

2 cups shelled edamame

Broth

2 cups vegetable broth

1 ½ TBS raw honey

2 tsp fresh grated ginger

½ cup soy sauce

1 TBS miso paste (optional)

Salt and pepper to flavor

Preheat oven to 425. Coat a baking sheet with sides with the 2 TBS oil. Add the parsnips, carrots and onions. Toss in oil and season with a sprinkle of salt and pepper. Roast the vegetables for 15 minutes in the preheated oven. Stir with a metal spatula and return to oven for 10 minutes. Remove when the vegetables are tender and beginning to brown.

While the vegetables are cooking combine the broth ingredients in a pan over medium heat. Bring to a simmer and turn down to low.

Divide the rice or barely into four bowls. Add ½ cup of edamame on top of the grain, then divide the vegetables up between the bowls. Pour the broth over each of the bowls. (Or put the broth in four cups or pitchers and allow each person to pour their broth over their bowl at the table). Serves 4.

Salads

Apple Spinach Salad with Orange Soy Dressing

Kale Salad with Warm Apples

Sweet Potato Salad with Horseradish Dressing

Quinoa with Pears, Cherries and Pecans

Greens with Chickpeas and Tomatoes

Sweet Potato Pomegranate Salad with Apple Cider
Pomegranate Dressing

Apple Spinach Salad with Orange Soy Dressing

This salad is high in magnesium, a nutrient many of us are deficient in. The richness of the avocado with the tartness of the apple and sweetness of apricots makes it a tasty winner! All your taste buds will be happy.

4 cups baby organic spinach leaves

1 avocado cut into small pieces

1 granny smith apple, cut into matchsticks

8 dried apricots sliced into fourths

½ cup pepitas (shelled pumpkin seeds)

Combine all ingredients in a bowl. Toss with dressing. (You may not use all the dressing). Serves 2 as a main course and 4 as a side salad.

Orange Soy Dressing:

¼ cup olive oil

2 TBS orange juice

1 TBS soy sauce

1 TBS red wine vinegar

Salt and pepper to taste

Combine all ingredients in a jar with a lid and shake.

Kale Salad with Warm Apples

When my college-aged daughter came home and ate a big bowl of this, I knew I had a winner. Who can resist warm apples in the fall? A key to this salad is allowing the kale to sit with the olive oil and vinegar for at least a half hour and even as long as overnight. Unlike lettuce, the kale needs the acid to help break it down so it isn't so tough.

Salad

6 cup chopped kale (1/2 inch pieces)

¼ cup olive oil

1 TBS apple cider vinegar

Apples

2 large apples, diced

2 green onions, diced fine

2 TBS butter

1 TBS apple cider vinegar

1 TBS raw honey (or regular)

¼ tsp nutmeg

¼ tsp ground ginger

Salt to taste

½ cup chopped pecans or walnuts

Chop the kale and set it aside in a large bowl. Drizzle the kale with the olive oil and apple cider vinegar. Lightly massage the kale with your hands. This step helps the kale break down. Let it sit for 30 minutes and as long as overnight.

In a medium sized sauté pan, melt the butter over medium heat. Add the apples and onions. Sauté for 2-3 minutes. Add the vinegar, honey, nutmeg, ginger and sprinkle with salt. Cook the apples for about 5 minutes until they are just becoming soft. Set aside to cool for about 10 minutes.

Toss the warm apples with the kale. Sprinkle with nuts. Serves 4-6.

Sweet Potato Salad with Horseradish Dressing

Right out of college I lived in North Carolina and I became enamored with southern food traditions. The sweet potato was one of those traditions. I've since become a huge fan of sweet potatoes for all their numerous health benefits, including: Vitamin A, magnesium, potassium, iron, fiber...the list goes on. While living in the south I ran across a recipe for Sweet Potato Salad with Virginia Peanuts and I was hooked. This is a healthier version of that original recipe, swapping out Greek yogurt for mayo and leaving the skins on for added nutrients and fiber.

1 ½ lbs. diced sweet potatoes, skin on (about 6 cups – or 3 large potatoes)

3 ribs celery, diced

½ cup peanuts (okay, just once I'll say roasted and salted are ok!)

½ cup plain Greek yogurt

1 TBS horseradish

½ tsp. sea salt

½ tsp. black pepper

In a medium pot filled with water, boil the sweet potatoes for 10 minutes. Drain into a colander and run cold water over them to cool. Transfer the sweet potatoes to a medium sized bowl. Add the remaining ingredients and stir gently to combine. Chill the salad for an hour or as long as overnight. Serves 6-8

Quinoa with Pears, Cherries and Pecans

Quinoa appears all over this cookbook and for good reason. It is a super food filled with not only plant-based nutrients but also protein. If you're a vegetarian, thinking about eating more vegetarian meals, or need to entertain a vegetarian, always keep quinoa in mind. The dried tart cherries add a delightful tang to this salad and the tart cherry juice used in the dressing has benefits that include anti-inflammatory properties that have shown to help reduce the symptoms of arthritis and muscle aches. And pears, with the skin on, provide a nice dose of fiber and pectin that helps toxins bind and flush from your body. And on top of all that..this salad is delicious on a crisp fall day!

1 cup quinoa, cooked according to package directions (2 cups yield)

1 pear chopped with skin on

½ cup dried tart cherries

½ cup chopped pecans

1 cup kale, chopped fine

2 ribs celery chopped

Tart Cherry Vinaigrette:

¼ cup olive oil

¼ cup tart cherry juice

1 tsp Dijon mustard

2 tsp red wine vinegar

¼ tsp sea salt

2 tsp honey

For Salad:

Cook the quinoa according to package directions. Set aside to cool or stick the bowl in the freezer for 10 minutes. Add the remaining ingredients. Toss with the dressing. Serves 4-6.

For Dressing:

Combine all ingredients in a jar with a lid. Shake well to combine.

Greens with Chickpeas and Tomatoes

Always adding those chickpeas! Yes I'm a huge fan of the garbanzo's amazing nutrient properties. And tomatoes last well into the fall in most climates. This becomes a hearty salad and is great served with a soup on a chilly fall night.

6 cups mixed greens (spinach, romaine, or spring mix)

1 15 oz can organic chickpeas, drained and rinsed

1 ½ cups chopped fresh tomatoes

½ cup raw sunflower seeds

½ cup chopped celery

2 green onions, chopped fine

½ cup pitted Kalamata olives

Combine all ingredients. Toss with dressing (on the next page).

Tomato Based Jazzy Dressing

My friend Bobbie taught me to add tomato paste to salad dressing. It adds an amazing sweet flavor to oil and vinegar based dressing. And this one gets its "jazz" from the addition of chopped Kalamata olives.

½ cup extra virgin olive oil

3 TBS red wine vinegar

1 TBS tomato paste

1 tsp. dried oregano

½ tsp sea salt

¼ tsp black pepper

1/3 cup pitted Kalamata olives

Combine all ingredients in a blender. Blend until smooth.

Sweet Potato Pomegranate Salad with Apple Cider Pomegranate Dressing

The perfect fall salad. Take it to your neighborhood open house, ornament exchange with girlfriends or served with a turkey sandwich Thanksgiving weekend!

4 cups sweet potatoes, peeled and cubed

1 cup chopped purple onion

2 TBS olive oil

Salt and pepper

1 cup pomegranate seeds

½ cup chopped walnuts

½ cup crumbled feta

4 cups salad greens or baby kale

Apple Cider Pomegranate Dressing:

3 Tablespoons Apple Cider Vinegar

3 Tablespoons Pomegranate Juice

1/3 cup olive oil

½ tsp ground ginger

¼ tsp ground cinnamon

½ tsp. soy sauce

Salt and pepper to taste

Preheat oven to 425. Coat a baking sheet with sides with the 2 TBS olive oil. Add the sweet potatoes and onions. Toss in olive oil and season with a sprinkle of salt and pepper. Roast the sweet potatoes and onions for 15 minutes in the preheated oven. Stir with a metal spatula and return to oven for 10 minutes. Remove from oven and let cool.

Once the vegetables are cool transfer to a large bowl and add the remaining salad ingredients. Toss with the dressing. Serves 4-6.

To make dressing: combine all ingredients in a glass jar and shake until well combined.

Sides

Brussel Sprouts with Kale, Fennel and Golden Raisins

Cauliflower Steaks with Spicy Curried
Roasted Pepper Sauce

Pumpkin Spice Butternut Squash with Farro and Apples

Twice Baked Garlic Sweet Potatoes

Brussel Sprouts with Kale, Fennel and Golden Raisins

It seems that if a recipe calls for dried fruit is it usually dried cranberries. I get tired of that. One of my favorite greens recipes was served at a family style Italian restaurant. It was loaded with golden raisins. I love this combination of plump golden raisins with the bite of brussel sprouts and kale.

1 clove garlic, minced

3 TBS olive oil

3 cups Brussel sprouts cut in quarters

½ medium onion cut in thin slices

1 fennel bulb cut in 1 inch pieces

Salt and pepper to taste

4 cups chopped kale

½ cup golden raisins

½ cup vegetable or chicken stock

1 tsp orange zest

1 TBS balsamic vinegar

½ cup pine nuts

In a sauté pan over medium heat, add the olive oil and garlic and onions. Cook for 3 minutes, stirring. Add the Brussel sprouts, fennel and salt and pepper. Cook for five minutes, stirring. Brussel sprouts may begin to brown. Add the kale, raisins and stock. Cover the pan and simmer for 5-8 minutes until kale and Brussel sprouts are tender. Add the orange zest, balsamic vinegar and pine nuts. Stir and cook another minute. Adjust seasoning with salt and pepper. Serves 4-6

Cauliflower Steaks with Spicy Curried Roasted Pepper Sauce

This cauliflower dish makes a lovely presentation. The Curried Red Pepper Sauce is perfect in the fall as the color makes a dramatic statement against the white cauliflower. I eat cauliflower every day. Really. It is my go to canvas as it stands up to so many bold flavors. And it is loaded with nutrients that have been shown to have cancer fighting properties.

6 - 8 wedges of cauliflower – or 4 cups florets

2 TBS coconut oil

Curried Red Pepper Sauce:

12 oz jar roasted red peppers – about 1 ½ cups

2 TBS tomato paste

½ tsp cumin

½ tsp curry powder

½ tsp garlic powder

¼ tsp coriander

¼ tsp ginger

¼ tsp cayenne pepper (optional)

Preheat oven to 450 degrees. Cut cauliflower head in half. From the middle area with the core still attached, make 4-5 half-inch slices. Then cut these in half. (If your cauliflower wedges fall apart or don't work out you can simply use the florets). Put the 2 TBS of coconut oil on a baking sheet. Pop it into the preheated oven with just the coconut oil on the tray. Leave it in the oven for about 2-3 minutes until the oil melts. Remove from oven and place the cauliflower steaks on the tray. Return tray to the oven. Bake the cauliflower wedges for 5-6 minutes. Remove from oven and flip the steaks over. Return to oven. Bake for another 5-6 minutes. Cauliflower should be a bit brown on each side. Remove from oven and top with roasted red pepper sauce. Serves 4-6.

While the cauliflower is baking make the sauce. Combine the roasted red peppers, tomato paste and all the spices in a powerful blender. Blend for about a minute until smooth.

Pumpkin Spice Butternut Squash with Farro and Apples

In the fall I always laugh at the onslaught of "pumpkin spice" donuts, lattes and cakes. The traditional flavors that we use with pumpkin pie don't always have to be combined with sweet foods. If you don't have all the spices for the "pumpkin spice" you can use a version that comes already prepared. But the extra can be used to flavor smoothies (see page 122) or other fall savory dishes.

2 TBS olive oil

4 cups butternut squash, cubed

1 onion, diced

1 cup diced tart apple

1 tsp. pumpkin spice blend

Salt to taste

2 cups cooked farro or barley or quinoa (all grains work)

2 tsp pumpkin spice blend

½ cup dried cranberries

½ cup toasted hazelnuts

Salt to taste

Pumpkin Spice Blend

5 TBS ground cinnamon
1 TBS ground ginger
1 TBS ground nutmeg
1 1/2 tsp. ground cloves

Mix together Pumpkin Spice Blend ingredients.

Preheat oven to 425 degrees. Put the olive oil on a baking sheet with sides. Toss the squash, onion and apple with 1 tsp. pumpkin spice and salt on the baking tray with the olive oil. Roast the vegetable mixture for 10 minutes at 425 and then stir. Roast another 5 minutes, stir. And then 5 more minutes. After 20 minutes the squash should be tender.

While the squash is cooking, prepare your grain. (Or if you're lucky maybe you have leftover grains like brown rice sitting around!) In a large bowl combine grain, 1 tsp. of pumpkin spice blend, cranberries and toasted hazelnuts. Add the roasted butternut squash mixture after it comes out of the oven. Toss well. Serves 4-6.

NOTE: To toast hazelnuts, place them on a baking sheet and bake in the oven for 2-3 minutes when the squash mixture is roasting. Watch VERY CAREFULLY. Nuts burn quickly.

Twice Baked Garlic Sweet Potatoes

Get over the garlic breath...these are to die for. And of course the health benefits of sweet potatoes and garlic have them both in my list of top 20 Superfoods! That list is in the back of my first book and I also have a popular presentation by the same name!

4 rounder sweet potatoes, and not too huge (the skinny ones are harder to work with)

1 head (yes the whole head) garlic

1 cup shredded cheddar cheese (optional)

½ cup non-fat Greek yogurt

2 TBS extra virgin olive oil, plus extra for baking potatoes

Sea salt and pepper to taste

Preheat oven to 350. Place each sweet potato on a square of aluminum foil. Drizzle with about a teaspoon of olive oil and a small pinch of sea salt.

Cut about a half inch off the top of the garlic bulb. Put the bulb in an aluminum foil square and drizzle with olive oil, just like potato.

Wrap up potatoes and garlic and pop them in the oven, sitting directly on the rack. Bake for 1 hour.

Remove potatoes and garlic and open up foil. Allow potatoes to cool enough to handle them.

Split the sweet potatoes in half and scoop out the middles, leaving ¼ inch around the potato skin. Put the scooped out potatoes in a large bowl. Transfer skins to a greased baking sheet.

Pull apart the garlic bulb and gently squeeze each clove so the roasted garlic pops out.

Put the garlic in with the potatoes. Add the cheese, Greek yogurt, 2 TBS olive oil and season with salt and pepper. With a potato masher, mash to combine. Fill the potato skins with the filling.

Return to oven and bake 10 minutes to melt the cheese and rewarm. Serves 6-8

Entrees

Mexican Quinoa and Flax Mini Loaves

Spaghetti Squash with Tomatoes, Spinach,
Olives and Feta

Coconut Pumpkin Curry

Sweet Potato Crusted Pizza

White Bean and Kale Stuffed Portabella Mushrooms

Mexican Quinoa and Flax Mini Loaves

These delicious mini loaves (if I called them muffins you may think they were breakfast!) are the perfect accompaniment to a salad, piece of chicken or even on their own. The flax seed not only helps bind the mixture together, but also offers healthy Omega 3 fats. The leftovers make an easy to pack lunch item!

1 cup quinoa, cooked according to package directions (yields 2 cups)

½ cup ground flax seed

1 cup chopped red bell pepper

½ cup frozen corn

1 cup shredded sweet potato, leave skin on

¼ cup canned green chilis

½ cup salsa

1 cup shredded cheddar cheese

1 tsp salt

1 tsp cumin

1 tsp chili powder

1 tsp garlic powder

2 eggs

Preheat oven to 375 degrees. In a medium bowl combine the ingredients except the 2 eggs. Stir to combine. Crack the two eggs into a bowl and stir with a fork. Pour eggs into the quinoa mixture. Stir gently to combine well. Coat 12 muffin tins with non-stick cooking spray. Using an ice cream scoop, fill the prepared muffins tins with a scoop of the mixture. Make sure the mixture is level with the top of the tin. Smooth the tops of the mini loaves. Bake for 25 minutes at 375. Allow the loaves to cool in the tins for 5-10 minutes before attempting to remove. Serve with hot sauce, salsa or guacamole. Makes 12.

Spaghetti Squash with Tomatoes, Spinach, Olives and Feta

You see the spaghetti squash and you know you can put tomato sauce on it and pretend it is spaghetti, but it isn't. Instead of hiding the squash, highlight it! Fresh chopped spinach and Mediterranean flavors help make the squash the star.

1 spaghetti squash

2 cups chopped spinach

1 cup chopped tomatoes

½ cup chopped Kalamata olives

1 tsp garlic powder

¼ cup good quality extra virgin olive oil

½ tsp salt

½ tsp pepper

½ cup feta cheese

Pepperoncini peppers (optional)

Preheat the oven to 400. Split the spaghetti squash lengthwise with a large knife. Scrape out the seeds. Place the squash face down in a glass baking dish. Fill the dish with a half inch of water. Bake the squash for about 45 minutes or until the skin has a little bit of give when pushed.

While the squash is baking, chop the spinach and tomatoes and place in a large bowl.

As soon as the squash comes out of the oven, hold onto each half with an oven mitt and scrape the middle of the squash into the bowl with the spinach and tomatoes. Add the remaining ingredients and stir with a fork. The heat from the squash will wilt the spinach. Top with additional olives and cheese. I also like a few pepperoncini peppers! Serves 6-8

Coconut Pumpkin Curry

Thai coconut curry is one of my all-time favorite flavors. The best "pumpkin" to use in this dish is the awkwardly lovely Kabocha variety. It is dark green, not too symmetrical but cooks into a sweet yet subtle flavor. If you can't find it, use Buttercup (similar but smaller in size) or Butternut, which is readily available. Curry powder almost always contains turmeric which has amazing anti-cancer and anti-inflammatory properties.

2 cups cooked rice

2 TBS coconut oil

2 cloves chopped garlic

1 large onion, diced

4 cups Kabocha, Buttercup or Butternut Squash

2 cups broccoli florets

1 14 oz can coconut crème (not coconut milk)

2 tsp curry powder

1 cup vegetable broth

½ tsp. red pepper flakes (optional – this will add a kick)

Sea salt to taste

In a large skillet with sides heat the coconut oil over medium high heat. Add the garlic and onion and sauté, stirring for 3 minutes. Add the pumpkin/squash and sauté stirring for another 3 minutes. Add the broccoli, coconut crème, curry powder, vegetable broth and red pepper (if using it). Simmer the curry for 10-15 minutes until your pumpkin/squash is tender. Serve over rice. Makes 4-6 servings.

Sweet Potato Crusted Pizza

Oh yum. I just love using sweet potatoes in a savory application. I know this isn't really pizza, and my kids give me a hard time when I tell them it is, but hey, it mostly resembles a pizza crust. Top with your favorites or use sautéed greens, wild mushrooms or caramelized onions. So many options.

2 medium sweet potatoes, peeled and shredded in food processor

½ onion shredded

½ cup shredded cheese – parmesan and cheddar work well

2 TBS ground flax seed

¼ tsp salt

2 large eggs

Non-stick cooking spray

½ cup additional cheese

Toppings of choice

Preheat oven to 400 degrees.

In a large bowl combine shredded sweet potatoes, onion, and ½ cup shredded cheese. Toss these ingredients together and add flour, garlic powder and salt. Crack the eggs into a small bowl and stir. Pour the eggs into the sweet potato bowl. Toss well to combine.

Coat a baking sheet with non-stick cooking spray. Pour sweet potato mixture into middle of tray and spread it out into a circle about ½ inch thick. Put in preheated oven for 20 minutes until the bottom begins to brown. Remove "pizza" from oven and slide a metal spatula underneath it to loosen.

Put on toppings and return to oven just until cheese melts, about five minutes. (or you can also put it under the broiler for a few minutes) Remove from oven, loosen bottom of "pizza". Allow to sit for 3 minutes. Cut into wedges and serve. Serves 2-4.

White Bean and Kale Stuffed Portabella Mushrooms

If you're a vegetarian, you're going to get served a portabella mushroom cap, stuffed with something! They are a blank canvas and mimic a piece of meat. So they become the easy out for someone who has to serve a vegetarian something. I get it. And I like a portabella too..but I like it stuffed with some superfood goodness. This rendition uses some classic Mediterranean flavors of tarragon, white beans and walnuts. Oh and kale...cause who doesn't love some kale?

2 cloves garlic, crushed

2 TBS olive oil

5 oz baby kale (6-8 cups)

1 15 oz can organic great northern beans, drained and rinsed

½ cup chopped walnuts

½ cup vegetable broth, divided

1 TBS dried tarragon or 2 TBS fresh chopped

1 tsp dried thyme or 2 tsp. fresh chopped

1 tsp sea salt

½ tsp black pepper

4 portabella mushroom caps (stems removed)

½ cup goat cheese or parmesan cheese (optional)

Preheat the oven to 350 degrees. In a medium skillet over medium high heat, heat the olive oil and add the garlic. Sauté about a minute, do not let the garlic burn. Add in the kale and sauté another minute. Add ¼ cup of the vegetable broth and the beans, walnuts, tarragon, thyme, salt and pepper. Simmer the mixture for 5 minutes.

Place the mushroom caps in the bottom of a ceramic baking dish. Fill each cap with ¼ of the bean mixture. Put ¼ cup of the vegetable broth in the bottom of the pan. Cover the dish with foil. Bake the mushrooms covered for about 35-45 minutes until mushrooms are tender. Top with optional goat cheese or parmesan cheese. Serves 4.

Chapter 5

Winter

Comfort food is winter food. And oh, it is so nice on a day filled with gloomy skies and dipping temperatures to walk into a kitchen and make those comfort foods. Soups, stews, and hearty flavors keep me functioning all winter. But so do winter vegetables like the root veggies that store well all winter and winter greens that boost our nutrient intake in the winter. Don't be afraid of winter produce, embrace the unique flavors of turnips, Brussel sprouts or cauliflower. Enjoy these recipes in front of a fire with someone you love.

Beginnings and Apps

Cranberry Walnut Dip

Cauliflower Pancakes

Spicy Eggplant Dip

Cranberry Walnut Dip

Cranberries get mistreated. We add a lot of sugar to these just because they're tart, but they don't need all that sugar. Cranberries have loads of vitamin C, magnesium, and high level of proanthocyanidins. These help reduce the ability of bacteria to cling to urinary track...making the cranberry a sought after remedy for UTIs. But let's just go with the fact that this dip tastes like the holidays! Spread on whole wheat pita chips or on top of fresh cut pears.

1 cup fresh cranberries

1 cup walnuts

3 TBS raw or organic honey

1 TBS balsamic vinegar

½ tsp sea salt

In the bowl of a food processor, pulse the cranberries and walnuts until they are well pulverized. Add the honey, balsamic and salt. Makes 2 cups. Serve with apples, pears or whole wheat crackers or pita.

Cauliflower Pancakes

I eat cauliflower every day. I just love the stuff. And it's a good thing, cauliflower is a member of the cancer-fighting cruciferous vegetable family. Research shows compounds in veggies in this group stop the growth of cancer cells. Another benefit comes from a compound in cauliflower called choline, a B vitamin that may boost memory and brain function. And I haven't even mentioned the digestive benefits and vitamins and minerals! These savory pancakes are delicious as a starter or served with a salad for a main course.

6 cups cauliflower chopped into small florets

1/3 cup hemp seeds

½ cup cheddar cheese

1 tsp. sea salt

1 tsp. garlic powder

½ tsp. black pepper

1 egg

3 TBS olive oil

Steam the cauliflower in a vegetable steamer or simmer in a small bit of water for 10-12 minutes until tender. Transfer the cauliflower to the bowl of a food processor and process the cauliflower until it is very fine. Transfer the ground cauliflower to a large bowl. Add the hemp seeds, cheddar, salt, garlic powder and pepper. Stir well to combine. Scramble the egg in a small bowl and add to the cauliflower mixture.

To cook the pancakes you can use one of two methods.

Stovetop: Heat skillet over medium high heat. Add the olive oil and wait until oil is hot. Form the cauliflower mixture into 2 ½ - 3" patties. Cook in the skillet for about 3-4 minute per side, until nicely brown on each side. (If you use non-stick cookware you can reduce the oil)

Oven method: Preheat oven to 425 degrees. Spray a baking sheet with non-stick cooking spray. Place pancakes on the sheet. Bake for 6 minutes, remove the baking sheet and flip the pancakes, bake for another 5 minutes.

Makes 12-15 pancakes. Serves 6

Spicy Eggplant Dip

It seems that most Mediterranean and Middle-East cultures have and eggplant spread that is used as an appetizer or spread. This one has no particular origin, just what sounded good to me at the moment I was making it! Eggplants contain fiber, B vitamins, copper and magnesium to name a few. And they have an antioxidant compound called chlorogenic acid that has cancer fighting properties and helps lower bad cholesterol. And this dish contains one of my favorite seasonings: smoked sea salt. Look in a specialty spice store or market for this wonderful salt that has been exposed to smoke. Leave the crushed red pepper out if you don't like the heat or add more if you love it!

2 TBS extra virgin olive oil

1 medium eggplant, cubed

1 large purple onion, chopped

Sea salt and pepper

2 TBS organic tomato paste

1 TBS apple cider vinegar

½ tsp. smoked paprika

1 tsp. smoked sea salt (use regular if you don't have smoked)

½ tsp. crushed red pepper

Preheat the oven to 350 degrees. On a baking sheet with sides, combine the olive oil, eggplant and onion. Toss with some salt and pepper to season. Bake the eggplant for 40 minutes at 350 degrees. Stir the vegetables at least two times during the roasting. Remove from the oven and transfer to a large bowl. Cover the bowl with foil or place the baking sheet on top of the bowl. Covering the vegetables for an additional 10 minutes allows the eggplant to steam and get soft. Transfer the eggplant and onions to a blender. Add the remaining ingredients to the blender. Blend until very smooth. Transfer to a bowl and serve with sliced vegetables, whole wheat pita or healthy chips. Makes 2 cups.

Beverages

Orange Digestive Dream Smoothie

Metabolism Monster Smoothie

Orange Digestive Dream Smoothie

Citrus fruit is generally abundant all fall and winter. And adding an orange to a smoothie is a wonderful way to get the fiber of the orange, not to mention the benefits of all that wonderful vitamin C. This smoothie is great for your digestive track as well. Ginger, kefir and flax seed all help add your digestive system and gut health. Half of your immune function takes place in your gut, so keeping it healthy in the winter is a key to good health.

1 orange, peeled

½ banana

½ inch piece fresh ginger

¼ cup kefir

1 TBS ground flax seed

3 ice cubes

Blend all ingredients on high in a blender until smooth. Serves 1.

Metabolism Monster Smoothie

Grapefruit has long been linked to weight loss. It contains an enzyme that may lower your insulin response. And more insulin roaming in your blood causes you to store weight. Fresh spinach also helps control blood glucose levels and is high in Vitamin K which many of us are deficient in.

Sections from ½ grapefruit

1 cup organic baby spinach

½ cup frozen mango

¼ cup frozen raspberries

¼ cup cucumber slices

Blend all ingredients on high in a blender until smooth. Serves 1.

Salads

Orange Pecan Brussel Sprout Salad

Arugula with Roasted Fennel and Dates
with Balsamic Dressing

Seared Romaine with Roasted Garlic and Lemon
with Lemony Parmesan Dressing

Veg-Head Salad

Orange Pecan Brussel Sprout Salad

At every holiday party there seemed to be a salad with oranges and pecans. The combination makes sense for winter because citrus fruits are in season. And Brussel sprouts shaved very thin are super tasty and have amazing health benefits including fiber, cancer fighting properties, reducing inflammation and supporting heart health.

4 cups Brussel sprouts

2 green onions, chopped

1 TBS grated orange zest

1 cup orange sections

1/3 cup extra virgin olive oil

2 TBS apple cider vinegar

½ tsp sea salt

Clean the Brussel sprouts and shred very thin. You can do this in a food processor with a slicing blade or a mandolin. If you don't have either of these options you can make this salad by chopping the Brussel sprouts very fine. Put the Brussel sprouts in a large bowl with room for tossing. Add the remaining ingredients and toss well. Serves 6

Arugula with Roasted Fennel and Dates with Balsamic Dressing

The spicy flavor of arugula pairs so well with the sweetness of the dates. And dates, because they are a dried fruit are available in the winter months. Dates are high in fiber, potassium and magnesium. But they are high in natural sugars so go easy on the snacking. They do make a great sugar substitute for baked goods as well.

2 fennel bulbs, sliced into 1" – 2" sections

1 TBS olive oil

Salt and pepper

1 cup walnuts, chopped

½ cup chopped dates

6 cups arugula

Balsamic Dressing:

½ cup olive oil

2 TBS water

2 TBS balsamic

1 TBS red wine vinegar

¼ tsp. salt

¼ tsp. pepper

½ tsp. dried coriander

For Salad:

Preheat the oven to 425 degrees. Coat a baking tray with sides with the 1 TBS olive oil. Add the sliced fennel to the tray and season with salt and pepper. Toss together. Roast the fennel for 10 minutes. Open the oven and stir the fennel. Roast another 10-15 minutes until it is beginning to brown on the edges. Cool the fennel to room temperature. Place the arugula in a large bowl. Add the fennel, walnuts and dates. Start with half of the dressing and toss the salad. Check to see if there is enough dressing and add more if needed. Serves 6.

For Dressing:

Combine all the ingredients in glass jar with a lid. Shake until the ingredients are combined. Store extra in the refrigerator.

Seared Romaine with Roasted Garlic and Lemon with Lemony Parmesan Dressing

A simple sear on the lettuce and lemon make for a very attractive and delicious salad. This is a bit like a Caesar salad but so much tastier! And the dressing is a nice change from fatty, chemical-filled bottled dressing. This is a great winter salad because the garlic is an immunity booster and the lemon helps boost your liver function. I have it as a winter salad for those reasons, but these ingredients are available year round so in the summer you can grill the lemon and lettuce outside.

1 TBS extra virgin olive oil

2 heads romaine lettuce, cut in half

2 lemons, cut in half

1 tsp. extra virgin olive oil

1 bulb garlic, (the whole thing not just one clove)

Lemony Parmesan Dressing:

½ cup plain Greek yogurt

2 TBS organic mayonnaise

2 TBS water

1 tsp garlic powder

¼ cup parmesan cheese

Juice from ½ lemon

Preheat the oven to 350 degrees. Cut the top off a full bulb of garlic. Drizzle about 1 tsp of the olive oil over the top of the garlic bulb. Wrap the garlic bulb in a piece of tin foil and put it directly on a rack in the oven. Roast the garlic for 30 minutes. Remove and let cool while still wrapped in foil.

In a medium skillet or preferably a cast iron skillet, heat the tablespoon of olive oil. Get the skillet very hot and place the romaine halves in, cut side down. You will probably have to do this in batches. Remove the romaine and place one on four plates. Do the same with the lemon halves. Getting a bit of sear on the cut side. Place a half lemon next to the romaine half on your plate.

Remove the garlic from the foil. Gently peel each clove out of the skin. If the top has been cut off enough the cloves should just squeeze out. Put 2 -3 cloves on top of each piece of romaine. Drizzle dressing over all tops of the salads. Serves 4.

Combine all ingredients in a small bowl. Stir well. Store extra dressing in the fridge for up to a week.

Veg-Head Salad

We tend to think of salads with lettuce, but an even more healthful version uses cabbage. I came up with this salad because I love my slicing blade in my food processor. I realized I could get my kids to eat many more vegetables if they were sliced paper thin. You can use whatever vegetables you have on hand. And the homemade Thousand Island dressing is a family favorite! The capers have a lower sugar profile than using prepared relish. (But in a pinch that works as well).

6 cups shredded cabbage (keep the pieces about 2-3 inches long)

1 carrot

3" piece of broccoli (use the stem if you like – it's tasty!)

3" piece of cauliflower

½ cucumber, cut in 1/4s before slicing

1 stalk celery

½ cup mushrooms

½ cup sunflower seeds

Put the cabbage in a large bowl. For each of the vegetables you use, make sure they are in chunks that will fit in your food processor or big enough to slice with a mandolin. Slice all the vegetables very thin. Toss them with the cabbage. Drizzle the dressing over the salad and toss.

Thousand Island Dressing:

½ cup plain Greek yogurt

2 TBS organic mayonnaise

2 TBS organic ketchup

1 TBS chopped capers

½ tsp onion powder

½ tsp salt

¼ tsp pepper

Combine all ingredients in a small bowl. This will keep for 4-5 days in the fridge.

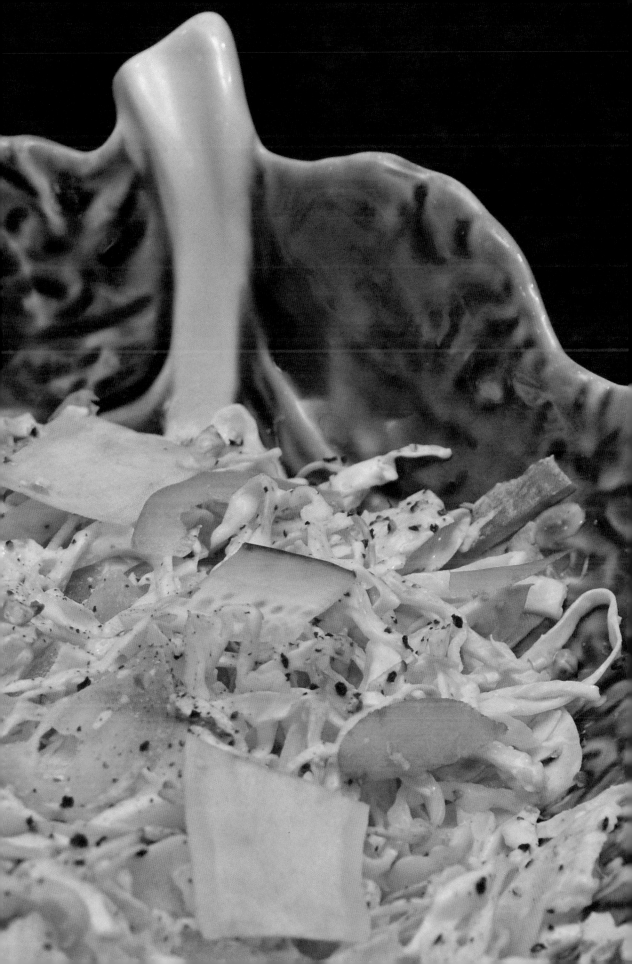

Soups

Split Pea Soup with Parsnips

Chick Pea Chili

Broccoli Cheese Soup

Roasted Tomato and Spinach Soup

Split Pea Soup with Parsnips

Are you stuck in a root vegetable rut? Tired of carrots? It is time to try some others. Root vegetables are beneficial because they grow in the dirt. They absorb minerals from the dirt! You absorb the minerals from them. Minerals like: iron, calcium, copper, magnesium and potassium. Many Americans are deficient in a bunch of those! And besides the minerals, parsnips contain antioxidants that have anti-inflammatory, anti-fungal and anti-cancer functions. And in this soup parsnips add a wonderful sweetness!

1 ½ cups green split peas

2 parsnips, peeled and chopped

2 carrots, peeled and chopped

1 onion, chopped

1 quart chicken or vegetable stock

2 cups water

1 tsp sea salt

1 tsp pepper

1 tsp dried thyme

Combine all the ingredients in pot over medium high heat. Bring to a low boil and reduce temperature to medium/low. Simmer soup for 1 to 1 ½ hours until vegetables are soft and split peas have all broken down. You may need to add more liquid if soup gets too thick. If you like a smooth soup you can blend the soup with an immersible blender or transfer soup to a regular blender. Blend for 1-2 minutes to make a smooth soup. This step is optional. Makes 6-8 servings.

Chick Pea Chili

We all love a good chili in the winter and creating a healthy version is super simple. For this version I soaked the dried chick peas overnight and then simmered them in water for an hour. This is an extra step, but using your own chick peas versus the canned give this soup really nice texture. But you can used canned as well. The soup gets thickened with the addition of a bit of quinoa. You can adjust the heat however you like by adjusting the chilis. I used one Anaheim chili. But if you are a bit afraid of heat, use a green or red pepper. You can also substitute a can of prepared chilis.

2 cups chick peas (either organic canned or dried that you have prepared as mentioned above)

3 cups vegetable stock

3 cups water

2 carrots, chopped

1 cup chopped onions

15 oz can organic chopped tomatoes

15 oz can organic tomato sauce

1 cup chopped chilies such as Anaheim or poblano (or canned green chilies)

2 tsp cumin

1 tsp garlic powder

2 tsp chili powder

¼ cup dried quinoa

1 tsp sea salt or to taste

Combine all the ingredients except the quinoa in a 4 quart sauce pan over medium heat. Bring the soup to a simmer. Simmer for 30 minutes. Add the quinoa and simmer on low for an additional 30 minutes. Serves 6.

Broccoli Cheese Soup

My kids love creamy broccoli soup from their favorite chain café restaurant...I don't. I can taste the preservatives and artificial flavors. Yes. They are in there. This is a lovely soup to serve on a chilly winter night. Make a grilled cheese sandwich and you have a happy family.

1 head broccoli, including stems, chopped fine (about 6 cups)

1 cup chopped onion

3 medium potatoes, peeled and chopped (about 3 cups)

1 quart vegetable or chicken broth

2 cups water

1 tsp garlic powder

2 tsp sea salt

1 tsp black pepper

1 cup cheddar cheese (optional)

Add all ingredients to a large pot except the cheese. Simmer over medium high heat for about an hour. Stir in the cheese. Transfer the soup to a blender or use an immersible handheld blender and process the soup until smooth, but with a few chunks of potato and broccoli left. Serves 4-6

Roasted Tomato and Spinach Soup

When I was in my 20s I worked near a café that had spinach tomato soup. I loved to stop in on my lunch break for a bowl. Imagine how disappointed I was when I asked one of the servers about the soup and she told me they bought in giant buckets. I set out to change that...and came up with my own version of the soup. Roasting the tomatoes before making this soup give it depth and sweetness all at the same time. And it is wonderful when combined with the nutrient-packed spinach.

2 cups grape tomatoes cut in 1/4s (alternatively you can use 2 large tomatoes)

½ medium onion chopped

2 TBS olive oil

Salt, pepper

2 15 oz cans organic tomato sauce

1 cup chicken, vegetable stock or water

2 tsp. agave nectar

2 cups chopped spinach

Salt and pepper to taste

Preheat oven to 400 degrees. Coat a baking sheet with the olive oil, add the onions and tomatoes, sprinkle with salt and pepper. Roast the onion and tomato mixture in the preheated oven for 15 – 20 minutes, stirring every five minutes or until onions are soft. While the tomatoes are roasting, add the tomato sauce, agave, spinach and stock to a medium sauce pan over medium heat. Add the roasted tomato mixture to the sauce. Simmer 10-15 minutes. If you like a little smoother soup, use an immersible hand blender to blend the soup. Or transfer soup to a blender or food processor and pulse briefly. Make 4-6 servings.

Sides

Roasted Root Vegetables

Turnip and Sweet Potato Anna

Quinoa Stuffed Acorn Squash

Stir Fry Broccoli with Sesame Seeds

Roasted Root Vegetables

If you haven't roasted winter root vegetables, beware. They are addictive and delicious. But also beware because parsnips and carrots are naturally high in sugars. So eating a heaping pile isn't advised, even though you'll want to. Keep your portion reasonable and just make them often!

2 TBS coconut oil or extra virgin olive oil

4 parsnips, peeled and cut in ½ inch chunks

4 carrots, peeled and cut in ½ inch chunks

2 sweet potatoes, peeled and cut in ½ inch chunks

1 large yellow onion, chopped

2 cloves garlic, minced

½ tsp sea salt

½ tsp black pepper

½ tsp garlic powder

Preheat the oven to 425 degrees. Put the coconut oil or olive oil on a baking tray with sides. Toss the vegetables with the seasonings and oil on the tray. Bake the vegetables for 10 minutes. Using a metal spatula, stir the vegetables. Return to oven and bake another 10 minutes. Stir again. Bake another 5-10 minutes until the vegetables are beginning to brown and turn tender. Serves 4 – 6.

Turnip and Sweet Potato Anna

An Anna is a casserole of thinly sliced vegetables. Usually it is potatoes, but this version is more nutrient dense with the turnips and sweet potatoes. If you haven't had a turnip recently, go on, try them. They are peppery and crisp and pair well with the sweetness of the sweet potatoes. But this can also be made with just sweet potatoes. The Anna cuts beautifully into wedges and looks enticing on a winter plate.

2 large turnips, sliced thin

2 large sweet potatoes, sliced thin

2 TBS melted butter

½ tsp dried thyme (or 2 tsp. fresh chopped)

½ tsp onion powder

½ tsp garlic powder

½ tsp sea salt

½ tsp black pepper

Preheat oven to 350 degrees. Combine the thyme, onion powder, garlic powder, salt and pepper in a small bowl. Set aside. Drizzle 1/3 of the butter over the bottom of a 9" pie plate. Layer half of the sweet potatoes on the bottom of the dish, overlapping slightly as you make a circle of the sweet potatoes. Take a pinch of the seasonings and sprinkle well over the potatoes. Drizzle a bit the butter over the potatoes. Next make a layer of the turnips. Again sprinkle with seasonings and then a bit of butter. Finish the Anna with the remaining sweet potatoes, seasoning and butter. Bake the Anna covered with foil for 30 minutes. Remove the foil and bake another 20 minutes. Remove and slice into 6 wedges. Serves 6.

Quinoa Stuffed Acorn Squash

I love an acorn squash in the winter. Really, there is no other squash that is such a blank canvas for flavor. It may have something to do with the size and the handy little pocket that is formed when you slice it in half. That hole in the middle is just crying out to be filled with some goodies. The protein in the quinoa makes this a filling dish that can even serve as a main course.

1 acorn squash, split in ½ and seeds removed

2 TBS butter

1 cup cooked quinoa

1 cup chopped onions

½ tsp dried thyme

1 tsp sea salt

½ tsp black pepper

2 TBS chopped fresh parsley

1 TBS butter

Preheat the oven to 350 degrees. Place the prepared acorn squash cut side down in a glass baking dish. Fill the dish with enough water to come about ½ inch up the sides of the squash. Bake the squash for 45-60 minutes uncovered in the oven. Remove from the oven and allow to cool for about 20 minutes.

Meanwhile heat the butter in a medium skillet of medium heat. Add the onions and sauté for about 6 minutes until they become translucent. Add the cooked quinoa, thyme, parsley and salt. Stir well.

Scoop the flesh of the acorn squash out of the cooked halves. Leave about a ¼ inch around the sides. Mix the acorn squash into the onion and quinoa mixture. Put the mixture back into the acorn half shells.

Transfer the squash halves to a baking dish. Divide the 1 TBS of butter in half and put a dab of butter on top of each half of squash. Cover the squash with foil and put back in the 350 degree oven for 20 minutes or until heated through. Cut the halves in half to serve 4 or serve a half per person as a main course. Serves 2-4

Stir Fry Broccoli with Sesame Seeds

Believe it or not, those tiny sesame seeds that some famous fast food chain throws on their buns, actually have health benefits. Sesame seeds and the sesame oil in this recipe are loaded with trace minerals like copper, magnesium and calcium. These minerals support vascular health, immune function, and even sexual health! And of course broccoli is loaded with vitamins and cancer fighting properties to name a few benefits.

1 head broccoli chopped, about 4 cups

2 TBS coconut oil

1 TBS sesame oil

1/3 cup chopped cashews

2 TBS sesame seeds

In a wok or skillet over medium high heat, heat the coconut oil. Add the broccoli and stir fry for 3-4 minutes. Then add the sesame oil and sauté another 3-4 minutes until broccoli becomes tender. Add the cashews and sesame seeds, cook another minute, stirring and then remove from heat. Serves 4-6

Entrees

Wild Mushroom and Barley Stew

Mushroom and Spinach Ragu over Creamy Polenta

Soft Tacos with Cabbage, Onions and Pinto Beans

Sweet Potato and Black Bean Enchiladas
with Creamy Cilantro Avocado Sauce

Lentil Stew with Eggplant and Capers

Wild Mushroom and Barley Stew

Mushrooms and garlic have amazing immunity boosting functions. And since many of us hit an immunity low in the winter, this is the perfect winter dish. You can substitute any grain or rice for the barley. The parsnips pair wonderfully with the earthy flavors of the mushrooms, so don't skip them!

1 TBS coconut oil

1 medium onion, chopped

3 cloves garlic, minced

2 large carrots, chopped

2 large parsnips, chopped

1 red bell pepper, chopped

8 oz shiitake mushrooms, rough chopped

1 cup instant barley

2 ½ - 3 cups vegetable or chicken broth

1 tsp dried thyme

1 ½ tsp dried tarragon

Sea salt and pepper to taste

2 TBS chopped parsley

Melt the coconut oil in a sauté pan with high sides over medium heat. Add the onion and garlic. Sauté, stirring for about 5 minutes. Add the carrots, parsnips and red pepper. Sauté, stirring another 5-10 minutes until vegetable begin to soften. Add the salt, pepper, thyme and tarragon. Add the mushrooms and cook another 5 minutes. Add the instant barley and vegetable broth. Cover the pan and cook for 10 – 20 minutes. Stir once to prevent sticking. You may need to add more broth depending on your brand of barley. (Trader Joe's 10 Minute Barley took 20 minutes and 3 cups of broth.) Sprinkle with parsley and serve with a green salad. Serves 4-6.

Mushroom and Spinach Ragu
Over Creamy Polenta

Eating for energy generally keeps simple carbs like corn to a minimum, but a little corn in the form of an organic corn meal is all good. Just make sure your veggies are in greater proportion to your polenta. This is a great recipe for winter as mushrooms and garlic are great immunity boosters.

1 TBS extra virgin olive oil

1 cup chopped onions

5 cloves garlic, minced

1 28 oz can crushed tomatoes (San Manzano preferably)

1 10 oz package cremim mushrooms, rough chopped

1 4 oz package shitake mushrooms, rough chopped

2 tsp Dried Italian herbs

1 tsp dried thyme

½ tsp black pepper

½ tsp sea salt

1 6 oz bag organic baby spinach (about 4 cups)

1 cup organic polenta (often found as 'stone ground' which is coarser ground)

½ tsp. sea salt

½ cup parmesan cheese

In a large skillet with sides, heat the olive oil over medium high heat. Add the onions and garlic. Sauté and stir for 2 minutes, watching carefully so the garlic doesn't burn. Add the tomatoes, mushrooms and herbs. The ragu will be quite thick with all the mushrooms. Bring the entire mixture to a slow simmer. Turn the heat to low and cover the pan and simmer for 20 minutes. While the ragu is simmering, prepare the polenta. Remove the cover and add the spinach. Stir until it is wilted. Remove the ragu from the heat.

For polenta:

Bring 2 cups of water to a simmer in a medium sauce pan. Add the ½ tsp sea salt to the water. Using a whisk quickly stir in the polenta. Continue to stir until polenta begins to pull away from the sides of the pan and is thick. Depending on the grind of your cornmeal this could take anywhere from 5 – 15 minutes. As soon as polenta reaches desired consistency, stir in the parmesan.

Serving:

Spoon about a half cup of polenta into a shallow bowl or onto a plate. Top with a cup of the ragu. Sprinkle with additional parmesan if you like. Serves 4.

Soft Tacos with Cabbage, Onions and Pinto Beans

This is a mid-western classic meats New Mexico flavor...and it is an amazing flavor winner! All over the mid-west a classic cabbage and noodle dish called Haluski shows up at any festival or event. This is my way of having the cabbage/onion flavor without the noodles or meat. Cabbage and onions both contain sulfur compounds that have been linked to boosting immunity and fighting off disease. A great thing to have during winter when we all can use a boost. And just like most authentic Mexican tacos, my tacos don't have cheese. A fried egg on top though adds the perfect comfort to this winter dish.

2 TBS butter

3 cups sliced onions (cut onion in half and then semi-circles)

6 cups shredded cabbage

1 tsp sea salt

1 cup diced butternut squash

½ tsp garlic powder

½ tsp smoked paprika

1 15 oz can organic pinto beans, drained and rinsed

6 – small corn tortillas

6 fried eggs (optional)

1 avocado, sliced

In a cast iron skillet (or other large skillet) melt the butter over medium high heat. Add the onions first, then the cabbage and salt to the melted butter. Allow to cook about five minutes then stir so all the cabbage hits the bottom of the pan. Continue to cook, stirring for about five minutes. Add the butternut squash, garlic powder and smoked paprika. Stir well and put a cover on the pan. Reduce the heat to medium low and cook for 10 minutes. Check it occasionally to make sure it isn't sticking. Remove the cover and add the pinto beans. Cook on medium low heat for another 5-10 minutes until the cabbage and onions are very limp and the squash is cooked through.

In another frying pan, cook eggs to your liking, either sunny side up or over easy. Set aside

Heating the tortillas:

Gas Range Option: Lay the tortillas, one at a time, directly on the burner grate. Turn the flame on medium and watch the tortilla closely. Just as it begins to brown on the edges, flip it using a pair of tongs. Set aside and continue with the remaining tortillas.

[Continued on next page]

Oven Option: Preheat oven to 425 degrees. Coat a baking sheet with non-stick spray. Lay the tortillas on the tray. Bake for 3 minutes. Remove the sheet from the oven, flip the tortillas over to warm on the other side.

Assembly:

Put a tortilla on a plate. Place about ½ cup of the cabbage/bean mixture on it. Top with a fried egg and a couple of avocado slices. Add a couple shakes of your favorite hot sauce and eat with your hands, and enjoy the mess! Makes 6 tacos.

Sweet Potato and Black Bean Enchiladas with Creamy Cilantro Avocado Sauce

I actually served these as a brunch item with a fried egg on top. And I had a guy who was used to bacon and eggs every day say, "If I saw this on a menu I would say 'no way', but this is a really good combination!" That is all the endorsement I need.

Enchiladas

4 cups chopped sweet potatoes – fine to leave skin on

½ cup chopped onion

1 chili pepper chopped, Anaheim or poblano (you can also use a can of chopped chilies)

1 15 oz can organic black beans

¼ cup organic plain Greek yogurt

½ tsp. sea salt

1 tsp. cumin

6 whole wheat or corn tortillas

Tomato Sauce

1 15 oz can organic tomato sauce

1 tsp cumin

½ tsp onion powder

½ tsp. sea salt

Creamy Cilantro Avocado Sauce

1 large ripe avocado

Juice from ½ lime

½ cup organic plain Greek yogurt

1 cup cilantro

Preheat oven to 350 degrees. In a medium sauce pan simmer the sweet potatoes for 10 minutes. Fill the sauce pan with about 2-3 inches of water and bring water to a boil. Drain the water from the sweet potatoes. Put three cups of the sweet potatoes in a food processor and puree. (Reserve one cup of sweet potato chunks to stir in later).

Transfer the pureed sweet potatoes to a medium bowl. Add the remaining 1 cup sweet potato chunks, chili pepper, black beans, yogurt, sea salt, and cumin. Stir well to combine. Set aside.

In a small bowl combine all the ingredients for the tomato sauce.

Assembly:

Spread ½ cup of the tomato sauce over the bottom of a 9 x 13 glass baking pan. Lay a tortilla flat and put ½ cup of the sweet potato mixture slightly off center. Fold the top of the tortilla over the mixture, fold in the sides, then roll up the tortilla. Lay the enchilada in the pan, seam side down. Repeat with remaining five tortillas. Spread the remaining tomato sauce over the top of each tortilla. Cover the pan with foil and bake for 30 minutes.

While the enchiladas are baking, make the Creamy Cilantro Avocado Sauce. Put all the ingredients for the sauce in a blender. Pulse until well combined and smooth.

Remove enchiladas from the oven. Garnish with a spoonful of Cilantro Avocado Sauce. Serves 6.

Lentil Stew with Eggplant and Capers

Hearty and warm, nothing beats a stew when the weather starts to turn cold. This one is excellent served with a green salad. The lentils offer a trifecta of health benefits: plant-based nutrients, fiber and protein.

1 TBS extra virgin olive oil

1 large purple onion, chopped

4 cloves of garlic, minced

1 medium eggplant, cubed

2 large carrots, chopped

1 28 oz can chopped organic tomatoes

2 TBS tomato paste

½ cup green lentils

1 cup vegetable broth

1 tsp sea salt

1 tsp black pepper

1 tsp dried thyme

1 tsp dried oregano

¼ cup capers

½ cup feta cheese (optional)

Heat the olive oil over medium high heat in a large skillet with sides. Sauté the onion and garlic for about 2 minutes. Stir so the garlic does not burn. Add all the remaining ingredients except the feta. Stir the stew and turn the heat down to low. Simmer the stew for 30 minutes, stirring occasionally. If it becomes too thick, add a bit more broth. Remove from heat. Dish into bowls and top with feta. Serves 6.

Thank You!

I want to sincerely thank you for browsing through my book, making a recipe, learning about a new food and sharing these foods with others. Nothing brings me more joy than sharing food, cooking food, eating whole real foods and helping other to feel their best! I hope this book has given you that joy as well.

I would love to hear from you! Tell me about a recipe you tried. Ask me a question. Or let me know that you're starting to feel more energetic! Email me at Kathy@KathyParry.com

And if you would like more resources to help you on your journey to feeling your best. Please visit my website at www.KathyParry.com to learn more. Don't forget to sign up for my monthly newsletter that always has additional recipes and inspirations. And please join me on Facebook and other social media platforms.

BUT there are even more ways to connect! If you have a group, event, association or business that is looking to be inspired, I speak nationwide on the subject of wellness. Learn about my programs at www.KathyParry.com.

Wishing you an energetic and delicious life!
Kathy

P.S. As a special bonus I've included two more sets of recipes. Living in a sports town like Pittsburgh, I'm always disappointed with the selection of food at most tailgates or game day parties. Skip the wings, nachos and cheese fries and take one of these **Tailgate Specials** to your next party. Another favorite gathering of mine is a **Holiday Brunch**. But egg casseroles are usually filled with meat or white bread. Skip those and try one of the recipes in the BONUS section.

Bonus Recipes

When you are trying to eat for an energetic life, certain events you attend may make it difficult! I know. I go to parties. I have people look at me and say, "What are you going to eat?" Well, I never go hungry. But I have learned that if I'm asked to bring something to an event, I always make something that I can eat. And in the process of doing that, lots of other people get to taste real, whole foods they may not have had before. So here are a few recipes for events that often don't have vegetarian choices.

The Tailgate

Words like greasy, fried and fatty describe foods you may find hanging out in the parking lots of stadiums in the fall. Why not go with foods that will really sustain your health instead?

Buffalo "Chick" Dip

This dip was in my first book, The Ultimate Recipe for an Energetic Life. It is so good and unique that I had to share it again. It seems that every tailgate or holiday party has a concoction known as Buffalo Chicken Dip. My kids love this stuff, but it is full of cream cheese and some renditions even use canned chicken. This is a vegetarian version that is so tasty even my teen aged kids eat it! Serve with celery sticks and cucumbers....oh and a few chips if you must.

1 15 oz can organic garbanzo beans, drained and rinsed

½ cup crumbled blue cheese

1 cup plain, non-fat Greek yogurt

¼ cup buffalo hot sauce
(I used Franks)

Put the garbanzo beans in the bowl of a food processor. Pulse until rough chopped. Add the blue cheese and pulse several more times, until fairly smooth. Add yogurt and hot sauce. Pulse to combine. Transfer to an oven-proof dish. Bake at 350 for 20-30 minutes. Serve with celery and pita chips. Makes 2 cups. The dip can also be served cold!

Black Bean Sliders

These are so fun and easy to eat when they are put in the middle of a crispy leaf of romaine lettuce. The flax seed is a great binder because it has healthy omega-3 fats that work well with the egg.

2 15 oz can organic black beans, drained and rinsed

1 small red pepper, chopped

½ cup chopped onion

1 tsp cumin

1 tsp chili powder

½ tsp sea salt (if you have smoked sea salt that is excellent in here)

½ cup ground flax seed

1 egg, cracked in a bowl and stirred

4 TBS olive oil or sunflower oil

12 romaine lettuce leaves

Chipotle Mayonnaise:

¼ cup organic mayonnaise

¼ cup organic plain Greek yogurt

1 TBS adobe sauce from a can of chipotle peppers

¼ tsp onion powder

¼ tsp sea salt

In the bowl of a food processor combine the black beans, red pepper, onion, cumin, chili powder and sea salt. Pulse until the mixture is well blended. Transfer the mixture to a bowl and add the flax seed and egg. Combine well. Chill the mixture for 30 minutes.

Heat a cast iron skillet or non-stick skillet over medium high heat. Add a TBS of the olive oil. Cook about 4 sliders at a time for about 4 minutes per side. These are a bit loose so flip them with some care. Transfer to a plate and repeat until all the sliders are cooked. Add more olive oil as needed to your pan.

Makes 12 slider-size patties.

To serve: put a slider on top of each romaine leaf and top with purple onion, tomato and chipotle mayonnaise.

Combine all ingredients in a small bowl.

Napa Slaw with Cucumbers

Slaws don't have to be loaded with mayonnaise to be tasty. This tangy slaw has an Asian flavor with the rice wine vinegar and cashews. The Napa cabbage is a bit milder than green cabbage and the texture is lighter as well. This salad is full of fiber and nutrients and gets even better after a night in the fridge. But be aware, if you do keep this until the next day, the cabbage absorbs a lot of the flavors and you may need to add additional vinegar or salt and pepper.

8-10 cups Napa cabbage chopped

4 green onions chopped fine

2 carrots, peeled and sliced thin

1 cup broccoli florets chopped small

2 cups thin sliced English cucumbers

½ cup chopped cilantro

1 cup raw cashews

½ cup olive oil

¼ cup apple cider vinegar

1/3 cup rice wine vinegar

1 tsp sea salt

1 tsp pepper

Combine everything in a large bowl or plastic bag. Stir very well to combine. Let the slaw chill for at least an hour and up to overnight. Serves 8.

Holiday Brunch

Breakfast meats, egg casseroles filled with white bread, and sugar-filled coffee cakes usually fill a holiday brunch table. And these are great traditions, but not so great when they help you feel sluggish the rest of the day. Try these brunch foods instead.

Eggs in Avocados

These are so fun! And they can be done in large quantity. Avocados are a superfood with amazing benefits for heart health, brain health, cellular energy production and metabolism.

4 ripe avocados

8 eggs

Salt and pepper

½ cup favorite salsa

Preheat the oven to 400 degrees. Cut each avocado in half and remove the pit. Using a small spoon enlarge the hole in the center of each half by removing about a tablespoon of the avocado flesh. (Reserve this for another use.) Place the avocados on a baking sheet. Put about a teaspoon of salsa into the hole of each avocado. Then crack an egg into each half. Some of the egg may spill over depending on the size of egg you use. Don't worry about it, your avocado will have plenty of egg. Sprinkle the egg/avocados with sea salt and pepper. Bake in the oven for 10-15 minutes or until the eggs are set. Remove and top with the remaining salsa. Serves 8.

Spinach Salad with Pears and Pomegranates

I just love the brightness both in color and flavor that pomegranates add to a salad. And the colors of this salad are seasonally appropriate if you're serving it at the holidays.

8 cups organic baby spinach

2 Bartlett pears, chopped skin on

Seeds from one pomegranate

1 cup chopped pecans or walnuts

Combine all ingredients in a large bowl and toss with the dressing. Serves 8.

Honey Dijon Dressing:

3 TBS white wine vinegar

2 TBS Dijon mustard

2 TBS raw honey

½ tsp sea salt

½ tsp black pepper

½ cup olive oil

Combine all ingredients in a jar with a lid and shake vigorously.

Sweet Potato Crusted Torta

While this lovely holiday brunch torta does have its share of cheese, just look at the other nutrient dense ingredients: sweet potatoes and escarole..yum. This is such a nice change from bread-filled casseroles.

Crust

1 large sweet potato, shredded

1 small onion, shredded

2 1/2 TBS flour

freshly ground pepper to taste and olive oil for brushing

Filling

1 TBS olive oil

1 onion, finely chopped

2 cloves garlic, minced

4 cups escarole, chopped in 1 inch pieces

1 TBS balsamic vinegar

6 eggs, lightly beaten

1/2 cup parmesan cheese, grated

1 cup provolone cheese, grated

2 tsp dried oregano

1 cup milk

Salt and pepper to taste

Crust:

Pre-heat oven to 400. Grate the sweet potato and onion. In a colander combine potatoes, onion and salt. Allow to drain for 15 minutes, then squeeze out excess liquid. Transfer to a medium bowl and add the flour. Press the mixture into a 10 inch pie pan that has been sprayed with non-stick cooking spray. Push half way up the sides to form a crust. Make sure potatoes aren't too thick. Brush with olive oil. Bake for 25 minutes until golden.

Filling:

In a skillet over medium heat, heat the olive oil and add the onions and garlic. Cook for 1 minute. Add the escarole and cook until wilted. Add the vinegar and cook 2-4 minutes longer. Transfer this mixture to the colander and press out the liquid. Allow to cool.

In a bowl, beat the eggs until well blended. In a smaller bowl, combine the cheeses. Add one cup of the cheeses, milk, and oregano to the eggs. Add the escarole mixture, salt and pepper to the eggs. Pour into the prepared crust and top with remaining cheeses.

Reduce oven to 375 and bake the torta for 45 minutes or until the center is set and the top is lightly brown. Allow to sit for 10 minutes before slicing into wedges. Serves 6.

Kathy Parry

About the Author

Kathy Parry is a professional speaker, author, mother of four and mildly addicted to dark chocolate. She loves to garden, although yearly fights a battle with a groundhog over her kale. When she isn't in the garden or kitchen, Kathy enjoys traveling. She is the author of two other books *The Ultimate Recipe for an Energetic Life* and *Hung Over, Sleep-Deprived, Over-Caffeinated and Living on Pizza*. (Both available at www.kathyparry.com and select online book stores.)

If you would like to bring Kathy to your company, group, organization or campus, give her a call at 412-427-1137. Kathy lives in Pittsburgh, PA.

Stay connected with Kathy by signing up to receive more recipes and inspiration at www.kathyparry.com

And follow her all over social media:

Facebook: https://www.facebook.com/KathyParrySpeaker

Twitter: https://twitter.com/KParryRealFood

LinkedIn: http://www.linkedin.com/in/KathyParrySpeaker

Pinterest: https://www.pinterest.com/RealFoodCoach/

Instagram: https://instagram.com/kathyparryrealfoodcoach/

Kathy Parry

Kathy Would Love to Meet You!

Need a Keynote Speaker?
Corporate Wellness Program?
Or Association Program?

Kathy Parry – You Real Food Coach will inspire your group in a fun and engaging program.

Kathy has spoken to hundreds of corporations, associations, colleges and clubs. With a mix of humor, information and inspiration, Kathy will take your audience on a journey to optimal health, energy and productivity. Her energy keeps audiences engaged and many participants start making healthful changes as soon as they leave the auditorium.

To Book Kathy Please Contact Her at:
Kathy@KathyParry.com
412-427-1137
www.KathyParry.com

What others are saying about
Kathy Parry's programs:

"We were fortunate to have Kathy present "The Secret to Ultimate Energy: a dynamic approach to a more productive workplace" at the DICK'S Sporting Goods Corporate Headquarters. Kathy's message was passionate, informative, and engaging. I am confident that a number of employees made significant changes to their lifestyle based on her coaching. I highly recommend her!"

Kristen Lane
Manager, Employee Wellness
Dick's Sporting Goods, Corporate Headquarters

Continued on next page...

"Kathy has an exceptional way of explaining the complex chemistry of our bodies in simple terms that help you to understand exactly how bad food hurts us and good food makes us energetic and happy. It was a real wake-up call!"

Mike V
Vice-President
PNC Bank

"This is the first in-service day when no one complained! My staff was talking for the rest of the afternoon about Ms.Parry's program and several told me it was the best programming I ever booked. Kathy engaged the group for over two hours and everyone left with a new attitude towards their health and energy levels. I can't wait to have her back!"

Michelle Zirngibl
Special Education Curriculum Leader
Upper St. Clair School District

Book Kathy Today:
Kathy@KathyParry.com
412-427-1137
www.KathyParry.com

Acknowledgements

So many people inspired me to write this book and I am so very grateful. But in addition to the inspiration, there was also an immense amount of support. I would like to acknowledge the following people:

To every single friend, family member or participant in one of my classes or presentations who ever said, "When are you writing a cookbook?" or "Can you give me a recipe?" Here you go! You inspired me and I thought of you while in the kitchen creating.

To Nancy Koch for the wonderful photographs in this book. You were truly wonderful to work with and captured the realness of my food.

To Weston Lyon and his team at PlugAndPlayPublishing.com for their amazing attention to detail in the publishing aspects of all of my books.

To Janice Wales, Merritt's caregiver and part time photo assistant, design consultant and recipe taster.

To my family for your always continued support. Dad, thanks for teaching me how to cook! Bill, Caroline, Heather, Tom, David, Maureen, Marti, Paige, JP, Graham, Merritt Joy, thanks for always, always being there for me.

And to Bryan my number one taster and kitchen crew.

Index

Salads

Apple Spinach Salad with Orange Soy Dressing	133
Black Bean Avocado Salad	36
Coconut Lime Quinoa Salad with Mangos	79
Greens with Chickpeas and Tomatoes and Jazzy Tomato Dressing	140
Kale Salad with Warm Apples	134
Lentil Salad with Chive Dressing	35
Marinated Green Bean Salad with Basil	84
Mixed Baby Greens with Blackberries	86
Orange Pecan Brussel Sprout Salad	171
Quinoa Salad with Zucchini and Tomatoes	82
Quinoa with Pears, Cherries and Pecans	138
Quinoa with Peas Dill and Feta	39
Roasted Fennel and Date Salad	173
Seared Romaine and Lemon Salad with Roasted Garlic	175
Spinach Salad with Pomegranates and Pears	214
Spinach Salad with Strawberries, Mangos, Pistachios and Mint	41
Sweet Potato Pomegranate Salad with Apple Cider Dressing	142
Sweet Potato Salad with Horseradish Dressing	131
Tomato Salad with Creamy Basil Dressing	80
Veg-Head Salad	176
Warm Spring Lentil Salad with Asparagus and Fennel	38

Soups

Asian Bowl with Edamame and Roasted Fall Vegetables	131
Asian Gazpacho	90
Black Bean Kale and Quinoa Soup	43
Black Bean, Corn and Farro Soup	129
Broccoli Cheddar Soup	181
Chick Pea Chili	180
Curried Red Lentil and Cauliflower Soup	127
Gingered Carrot and Lentil Soup	47
Golden Beet and Yellow Pepper Soup	89
Italian White Bean and Tomato	130
Pea with Parsnips Soup	179

Potato Leek Soup	45
Roasted Tomato Spinach Soup	182
Spicy Cold Cucumber Soup with Avocado	44

Sides

Asparagus with Leeks and Sugar Snap Peas	49
Bok Choy with Coconut Oil and Tumeric	96
Brussel Sprouts with Kale, Fennel and Golden Raisins	145
Cauliflower Steaks with Spicy Curried Pepper Sauce	147
Green Beans with Lemon, Garlic and Walnuts	100
Jicama Mango Slaw	50
Napa Cabbage and Cucumber Slaw	210
Pumpkin Spice Butternut Squash with Farro and Apples	148
Quinoa Stuffed Acorn Squash	188
Quinoa with Roasted Vegetables and Capers	51
Roasted Root Vegetables	185
Spring Peas with Vidalia Onions and Mushrooms	52
Stir Fry Broccoli with Sesame Seeds and Cashews	190
Swiss Chard with Olives and Roasted Red Peppers	95
Turnip and Sweet Potato Anna	186
Twice Baked Sweet Potatoes	149
Yellow Squash Bake	99

Entrees

Bean Sliders	
Cannellini Beans and Greens	55
Cauliflower Crusted Vegetable Shepherds Pie	60
Chickpea burgers with Cilantro Tahini Yogurt Sauce	103
Coconut Pumpkin Curry	155
Eggs in Avocado Halves with Salsa	213
Enchiladas with Sweet Potatoes and Black Beans	199
Kale and Rice Stuffed Poblano Peppers with Chipotle Sauce	58
Lentil Stew with Eggplant and Capers	200
Mexican Quinoa and Flax Mini Loaves	151
Mushroom and Spinach Ragu over Creamy Polenta	195
Mushroom Barley Stew	193
Roasted Summer Vegetable Lasagna with Pesto Filling	104

Sauces and Dressings: